Natural Resource Condition Assessment

City of Rocks National Reserve – Research Natural Area

Natural Resource Technical Report NPS/UCBN/NRTR—2010/299

Jack Bell
Northwest Management, Inc.
PO Box 9748
Moscow, Idaho 83843

Drake Barton
Northwest Management, Inc.
503 State Street
Helena, Montana 59601

March 2010

U.S. Department of the Interior
National Park Service
Natural Resource Program Center
Fort Collins, Colorado

The National Park Service, Natural Resource Program Center publishes a range of reports that address natural resource topics of interest and applicability to a broad audience in the National Park Service and others in natural resource management, including scientists, conservation and environmental constituencies, and the public.

The Natural Resource Technical Report Series is used to disseminate results of scientific studies in the physical, biological, and social sciences for both the advancement of science and the achievement of the National Park Service mission. The series provides contributors with a forum for displaying comprehensive data that are often deleted from journals because of page limitations.

All manuscripts in the series receive the appropriate level of peer review to ensure that the information is scientifically credible, technically accurate, appropriately written for the intended audience, and designed and published in a professional manner. This report received informal peer review by subject-matter experts who were not directly involved in the collection, analysis, or reporting of the data. Data in this report were collected and analyzed using methods based on established, peer-reviewed protocols and were analyzed and interpreted within the guidelines of the protocols.

Views, statements, findings, conclusions, recommendations, and data in this report are those of the author(s) and do not necessarily reflect views and policies of the National Park Service, U.S. Department of the Interior. Mention of trade names or commercial products does not constitute endorsement or recommendation for use by the National Park Service.

This report is available from Pacific Regional Office and the Natural Resource Publications Management website (http://www.nature.nps.gov/publications/NRPM).

Please cite this publication as:

NPS 003/101512, March 2010

Contents

Contents

Figures

Figures

Tables

Appendixes

Acknowledgements

We wish to begin by thanking Cheryl Teague, Landscape Architect, and Marsha Davis, Geologist, of the National Park Service Pacific West Regional Office for initiating the project and their time and courteous help at all stages of work. Ms. Teague was extremely helpful providing guidance and information to the authors on key issues surrounding the City of Rocks National Reserve and Research Natural Area. We owe a great deal of appreciation to the hard work of the field crew, Drake Barton and Kathy Elliot, Northwest Management, Inc. Vaiden Bloch, GIS Specialist, with Northwest Management, Inc. was invaluable in preparing the Geodatabase and map project files. Finally, we are very thankful for all the support and help from Lisa Garrett and Gordon Dicus, National Park Service - Upper Columbia Basin Network, and Wallace Keck, City of Rocks National Reserve, for data and editorial assistance.

Executive Summary

The assessment report and accompanying geodatabase is designed to give the managers and planners of the City of Rocks National Reserve (CIRO) a better understanding of the natural resources within the Research Natural Area (RNA). Assessment of the natural resources was accomplished by conducting literature reviews, evaluating existing data, and collection of new data. The CIRO was created November 18, 1988, by Public Law 100-696, Arizona-Idaho Conservation Act of 1988. This act drew a 22 mile boundary around lands owned or managed by the USDA Forest Service (USFS), Bureau of Land Management (BLM), Idaho Department of Parks and Recreation (IDPR), and private individuals. After the approval of the *1994 City of Rocks National Reserve Comprehensive Management Plan,* the Park Service officially transferred on-site management of the reserve to IDPR on May 2, 1996.

Prior to creation of CIRO in 1988 the City of Rocks RNA was established by the BLM through the Amendment to the 1985 *Cassia Resource Management Plan* and by the 1987 USFS *Sawtooth National Forest Land and Resource Management Pla*n. The 312 acre RNA is composed of 240 acres from the BLM and 72 acres from the USFS.

A rapid assessment method co-developed by the Natural Resources Conservation Service (NRCS), Agricultural Research Service (ARS), BLM, and the United States Geological Survey (USGS) was used to evaluate the health of two sites in the RNA. The method is described in the publication "Interpreting Indicators of Rangeland Health" (Pellant et al. 2005). The methodology is based on the potential of land to produce distinctive kinds, amounts, and proportions of vegetation and evaluates 3 major landscape processes; soil stability, hydrologic function, and biologic integrity.

A field survey of the RNA was conducted during the week of July 20 through July 24, 2009. The survey consisted of compilation of a plant species list, search for rare and endangered plants, and a list of all mammals, birds, and reptiles recorded based on signs or visual sightings. Human impacts were noted, particularly evidence of grazing or mining. Given the significance of the singleleaf pinyon (*Pinus monophylla*) to the RNA, several large trees were sized and aged. Twenty-seven assessment points were recorded with global positioning systems (GPS) and representative pictures taken of important features. A vegetation map developed from data collected in 2009 and in draft form was used to analyze the distribution of vegetation within the RNA and a proposed extension area.

The two rapid assessment sites had minor amounts of cheatgrass (*Bromus tectorum*) and very few non-native forbs. The sites are in very good condition and functioning properly in all three major landscape processes based on the evaluation. From the field survey, 211 plants species were identified out of the 533 species listed for CIRO. There was no evidence of any listed threatened, endangered, or sensitive plant species. Singleleaf pinyon – Utah juniper (*Juniperus osteosperma*) plant associations account for 36.7% of the RNA. Bare ground/rocks account for 25.1% and is spatial intermixed with the vegetation. The ages of large trees in the RNA were determined for four singleleaf pinyon and one limber pine (*Pinus flexilis*) and varied from 310 to 410 years of age. No evidence was found for any listed or candidate wildlife species in the RNA.

The only human impacts noted in the RNA were from cattle grazing along the southern and western boundaries. The boundary between the two active grazing allotments is described as a natural boundary and current maps show areas of overlap with the RNA. NPS guidelines for RNA management prohibit cattle grazing, which would require action by CIRO to correct this condition, either through fencing or other management actions. No other human or natural disturbances were noted in the RNA. Recreation activities adjacent to the RNA include rock climbing, hiking, mountain bike riding, and horseback riding on a series of maintained trails.

The CIRO RNA can meet the objectives for RNAs defined in *Natural Resource Management Guidelines NPS-77* with proper management. The RNA is an excellent reference site for monitoring the effects of management actions in similar sites outside the RNA. It also could provide baseline data for long-term monitoring of natural changes, such as wildfire and climate change, in the singleleaf pinyon community. The RNA preserves a healthy old-growth stand of singleleaf pinyon at the northern-most distribution of the species and associated community. The RNA will preserve the genetic diversity of the singleleaf pinyon community. The CIRO RNA is one of four RNA's in Idaho with a singleleaf pinyon plant association.

A 170 acre expansion of the RNA along the western boundary is proposed based on the similarity of vegetation and rock outcrops found in the RNA. An expansion of the RNA into this area would require structures to restrict cattle grazing, modifications to grazing management plans, and restrictions on recreation use. Further research would be required to determine if the expansion area meets all the requirements for a RNA, including possible changes to plant communities due to cattle grazing. Also proposed is an adjustment to the current RNA boundary that would incorporate the natural boundaries of the Graham Creek and Circle Creek allotments. The adjustment would create a 350 acre RNA and would have similar vegetation composition as the current RNA. Expansion or adjustment of the RNA could conflict with other management goals and objectives for CIRO not considered in this report.

Introduction

Purpose and Scope

The City of Rocks National Reserve (CIRO) was created November 18, 1988, by Public Law 100-696, Arizona-Idaho Conservation Act of 1988. The Act drew a 22 mile boundary around lands owned or managed by the USDA Forest Service (USFS), Bureau of Land Management (BLM), Idaho Department of Parks and Recreation (IDPR), and private individuals. After the approval of the *1994 City of Rocks National Reserve Comprehensive Management Plan,* the National Park Service (NPS) officially transferred on-site management of the reserve to the IDPR on May 2, 1996.

Prior to creation of CIRO in 1988 the City of Rocks Research Natural Area (RNA) was established by the BLM through amendment to the 1985 *Cassia Resource Management Plan* and by the 1987 USFS *Sawtooth National Forest Land and Resource Management Pla*n. The 312 acre RNA is composed of 240 acres from the BLM and 72 acres from the USFS.

In the fall of 2009 the NPS began the process of creating a General Management Plan (GMP) for CIRO. The GMP will serve as a guidebook to help managers make decisions on how to protect resources, what levels and types of uses are appropriate, what types of facilities should be developed, and how people should access the CIRO. Everything in the GMP must be consistent with the CIRO's purpose and significance The GMP also must meet the requirements of the legislation that established the NPS in 1916 that states the NPS must protect a park's natural and cultural resources while inviting appropriate visitor use and enjoyment. To assist in the development of the GMP, a natural resource condition assessment (NRCA) was conducted on the RNA.

An NRCA is a broad-scope ecological assessment intended to synthesize "information products" readily usable by park managers for resource stewardship planning and reporting performance measures such as the Department of the Interior Strategic Plan's "land health" goals. Three elements are important to making these assessments useful for both planning and performance reporting:

1. Build on data, information, and knowledge already assembled through efforts of the NPS Inventory and Monitoring Program, NPS science support programs, and from partner collaborators working in and near parks;

2. Utilize a strong geospatial component for examination of existing data, analyzing information, and presentation of the results in map and digital form;

3. Provide narrative and/or semi-quantitative descriptions of science-based reference conditions for park resources that will assist parks as they work to define Desired Future Conditions through park planning processes. These reference conditions will become more refined and quantitative over time.

Information gained from this report will form the basis for development of actions to reduce and prevent impairment of park resources through park and partnership efforts. The purpose and uses of the NRCA are to assist in:

- Near-term strategic planning to allocate limited staff and budget resources toward high priority (relatively more significant or vulnerable) park-managed lands;

- General Management Plan and Resource Stewardship Strategy development, which represents the planning process that formalizes park management zones, desired condition management objectives, and associated measurement indicators and targets;

- Park reporting to the Department of Interior's "land health goals" and to an Office of Management and Budget "resource condition scorecard";

- Park efforts to communicate and partner with other stakeholders in order to address watershed or landscape scale resource management issues.

This report is designed to give park staff a moment-in-time assessment of the natural resources of the RNA. The objectives for this project are to:

- Provide a vegetative and wildlife assessment for the RNA

- Document resource impacts within the RNA

- Describe any uses that would be compatible with RNA designation

- Recommend other areas within the park for designation due to biological diversity

Study Area

History

CIRO is located in the Albion Mountains of the Northern Great Basin in Idaho and is a unique geologic area with granite pinnacles and monoliths. The area has long been an oddity and wonder, especially for emigrants traveling the California Trail (1843-1869). One emigrant artist, James F. Wilkins, named the area that contained these geologic features the City of Rocks in 1849. By the 1870s, only a few ranchers and farmers had settled in the surrounding area (including Almo and Junction Valley, Idaho). A 1931 report on the geologic and mineral resources of the eastern half of Cassia County recommended the best use for the City of Rocks was as a national monument (Anderson 1931). The Idaho Legislature declared Section 36 within City of Rocks as a state park under the jurisdiction of the Idaho Lands Board on February 27, 1957. In 1964 it was designated a national historic landmark. On March 15, 1973, Section 36 was transferred to the Idaho Department of Parks and Recreation (IDPR) from the Department of Lands. The following year, the area was designated a national natural landmark.

The 14,407 acres of CIRO protect a 6.2 mile segment of the congressionally designated California National Historic Trail and the surrounding cultural landscape (Figure 1). The CIRO landscape also includes a portion of the Salt Lake Alternate (of the California Trail), Mormon

Battalion Trail, Kelton-Boise Stage Route, remnant trail ruts, and emigrant signatures written with axle grease on prominent rock features. Other cultural resources include prehistoric artifacts, homesteads, irrigation and ranching improvements, and mica mines. There has been a history of cattle grazing on public and private lands in and around CIRO that continues today on seven authorized allotments.

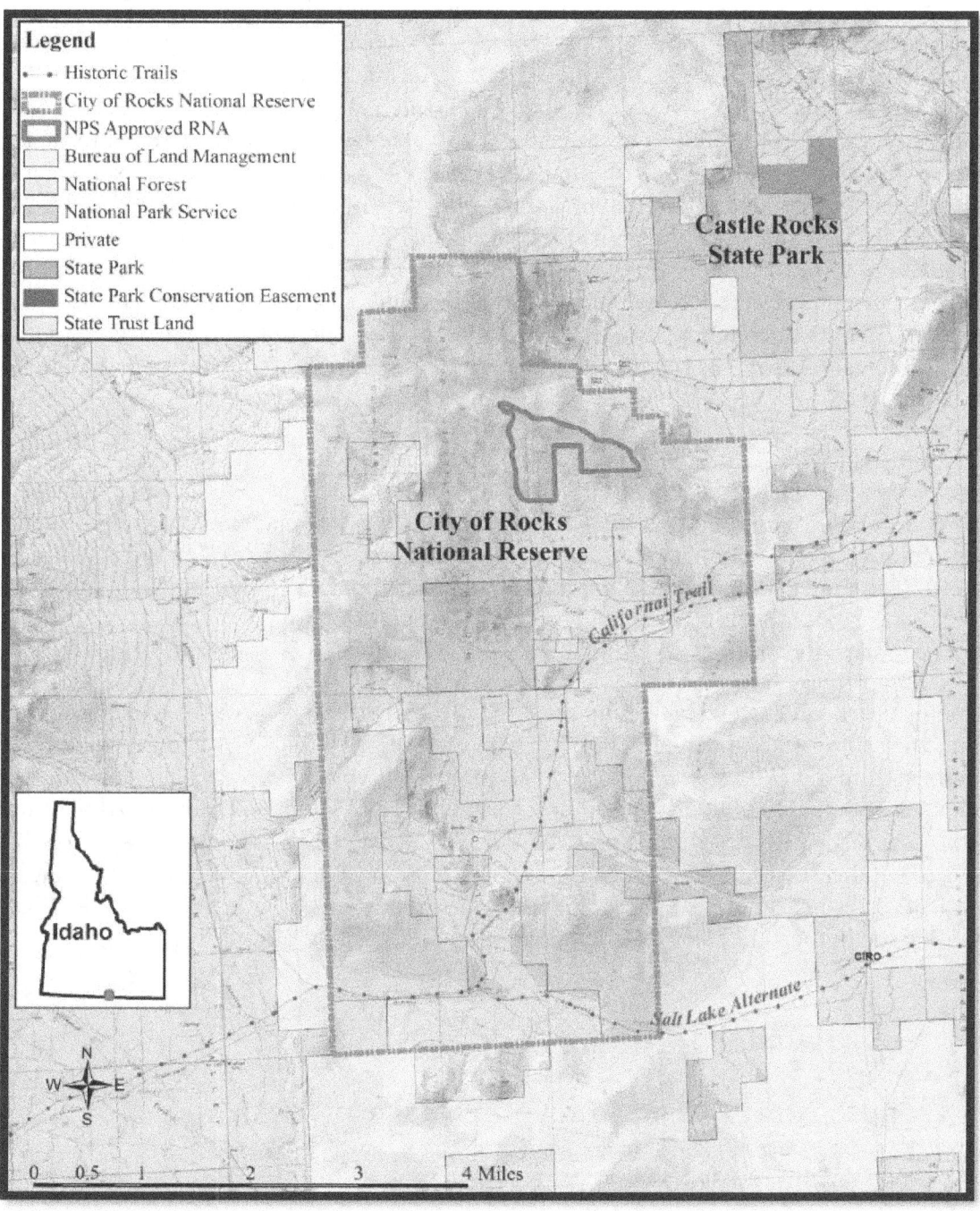

Figure 1. Map of land ownership in CIRO and the surrounding area.

RNA's are defined as "…part of a national network of sites designed to facilitate research and preserve natural features" (NPS 2004). They usually represent prime examples of ecological communities that have little past disturbance and have unimpeded natural processes. RNA's are permanently set aside and managed exclusively for long-term non-manipulative research and educational activities (NPS 2004).

In the late 1970s, the Idaho Natural Areas Coordinating Committee (INACC), funded by The Nature Conservancy, identified potential RNA's on BLM and USFS lands in Idaho (Wellner and Johnson 1974). The INACC first identified a 640 acre area in CIRO for approval as a RNA on USFS managed lands in a 1979 report to the USFS (Bal and Wellner 1979). A similar report was submitted to the BLM in 1983 for establishing a 240 acre RNA on lands adjacent to USFS lands (Caicco and Wellner 1983). Based on the INACC recommendations the BLM established a 240 acre RNA/Area of Critical Environmental Concern (ACEC) in 1988 (BLM 1987). The USFS designated a smaller area (45 acres) than recommended by the INACC in 1987 (USFS 1987) due to the inability to limit cattle grazing on the larger area. The USFS did not formally approve the RNA. The current 312 acre RNA (240 acres of BLM and 72 acres of USFS) was identified in the November 7, 1990 letter and report (Bal and Wellner 1979) submitted to Steve Culver of the NPS by Charles Wellner. Figure 2 displays a map of the proposed boundaries and approved RNA for CIRO.

The NPS officially recognized the 312 acre boundary for the RNA at CIRO in the *Comprehensive Management Plan* (NPS 1995). The Plan states the RNA will be managed under the NPS *Natural Resource Management Guidelines NPS-77*. Management activities were limited to non-manipulative research and/or education and it specifically states grazing is not allowed in the RNA. The Plan also states there was approximately 100 acres, not defined on a map, lying to the west of the current boundary being considered for addition to the RNA. The additional lands were a portion of the original USFS lands identified by Bal and Wellner (1979).

The major justification for establishing the CIRO RNA was to preserve the exceptional geological features (Bal and Wellner 1979). The vegetation in the RNA is dominated by stands of singleleaf pinyon (*Pinus monophylla*)-Utah juniper (*Juniperus osteosperma*) woodlands, which is representative of the northern limit for the range of singleleaf pinyon. At the time there were no established RNA's for this plant community. Rust (1996) inventoried and classified 12 RNA's in southeast Idaho that were dominated by pinyon-juniper and juniper woodlands. Only 4 of the 12 RNA's had singleleaf pinyon in the plant communities (Figure 3) with the CIRO RNA containing the highest frequency of singleleaf pinyon in sample plots (Rust 1996).

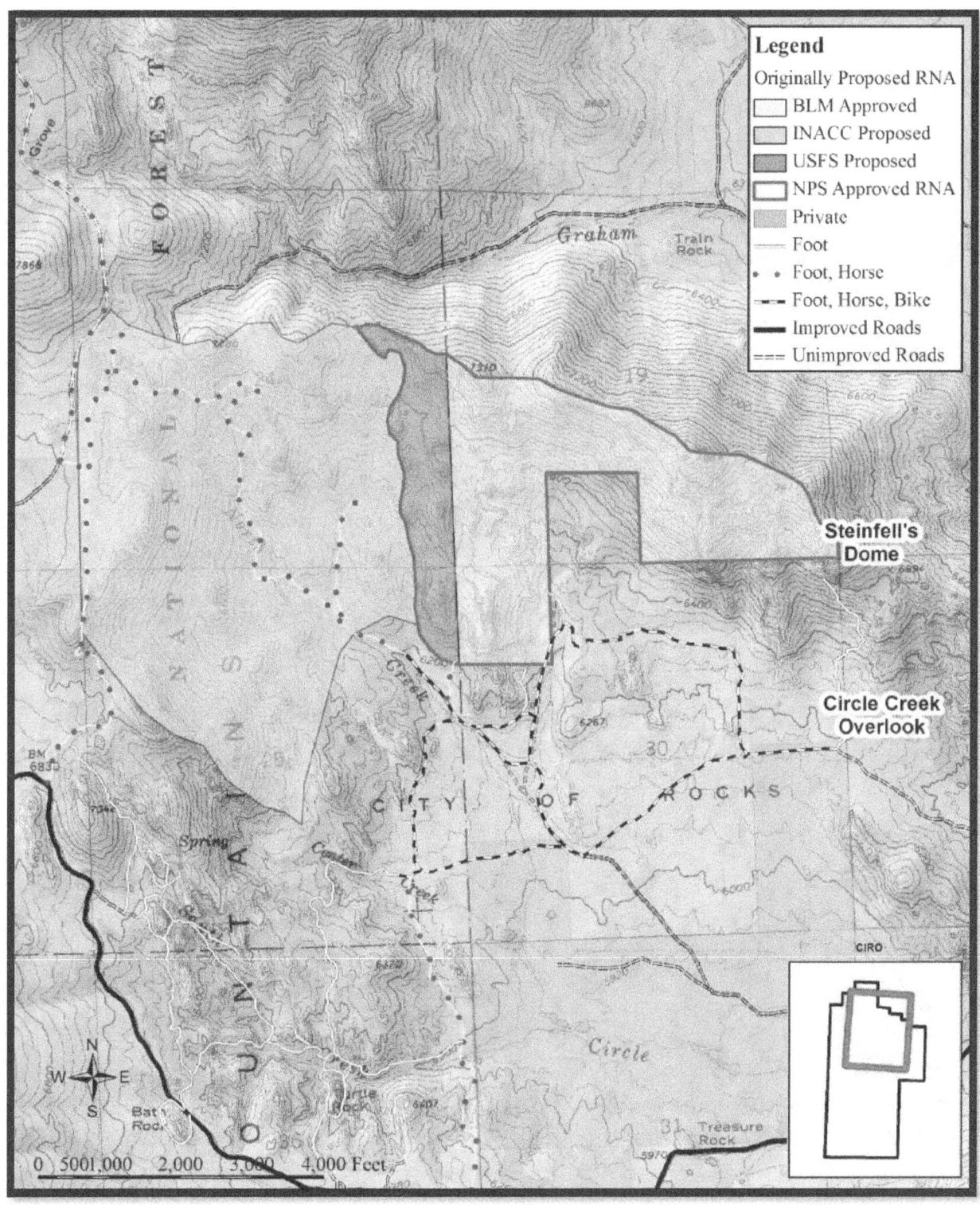

Figure 2. Map of the originally proposed RNA boundaries by Idaho Natural Areas Coordinating Committee (INACC) and approved by the BLM, USFS, and NPS.

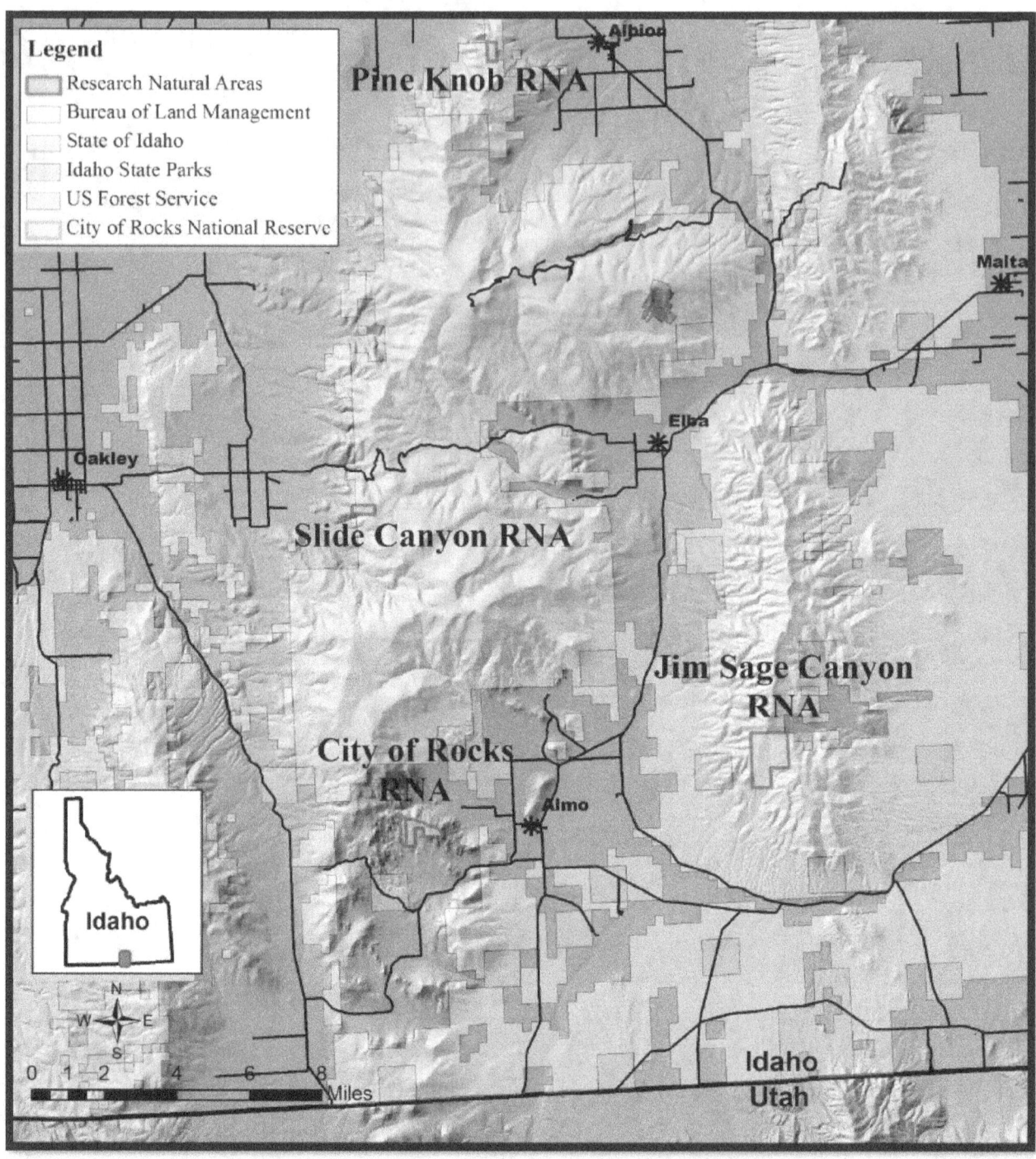

Figure 3. Map of the 4 RNAs in Idaho with singleleaf pinyon-Utah juniper as a major component of the woodland plant community.

RNA Setting

The CIRO RNA is located in the southern part of the Albion Mountains and in the northern end of the Great Basin physiographic province. Geologic features dominate the RNA and surrounding Circle Creek basin. The geology is composed mainly of the Green Creek complex, a 2.5 billion year old granitic gneiss basement rock with the Almo pluton, granitic-type rock, intruding through the older complex about 25 to 30 million years ago (Pogue 2008). The RNA is located in the northern portion of the Circle Creek basin (Figure 4). The basin is characterized by steep-sided, smooth and rounded bedrock knobs known as bornhardts. They are small-scale, granite-gneiss domes that form by granular disintegration along joints. Most bornhardts have formed in the Almo pluton, but some are also in the Green Creek complex. The RNA lies along the northern side of Circle Creek basin where several bornhardts and exposed bedrock form a crescent-shaped wall that is the highest elevation in the basin. Smaller and more isolated knobs protrude from the floor of Circle Creek basin. Elevation in the RNA ranges from 6,200 feet at the southern boundary to 7,688 feet along the ridge on the northern border

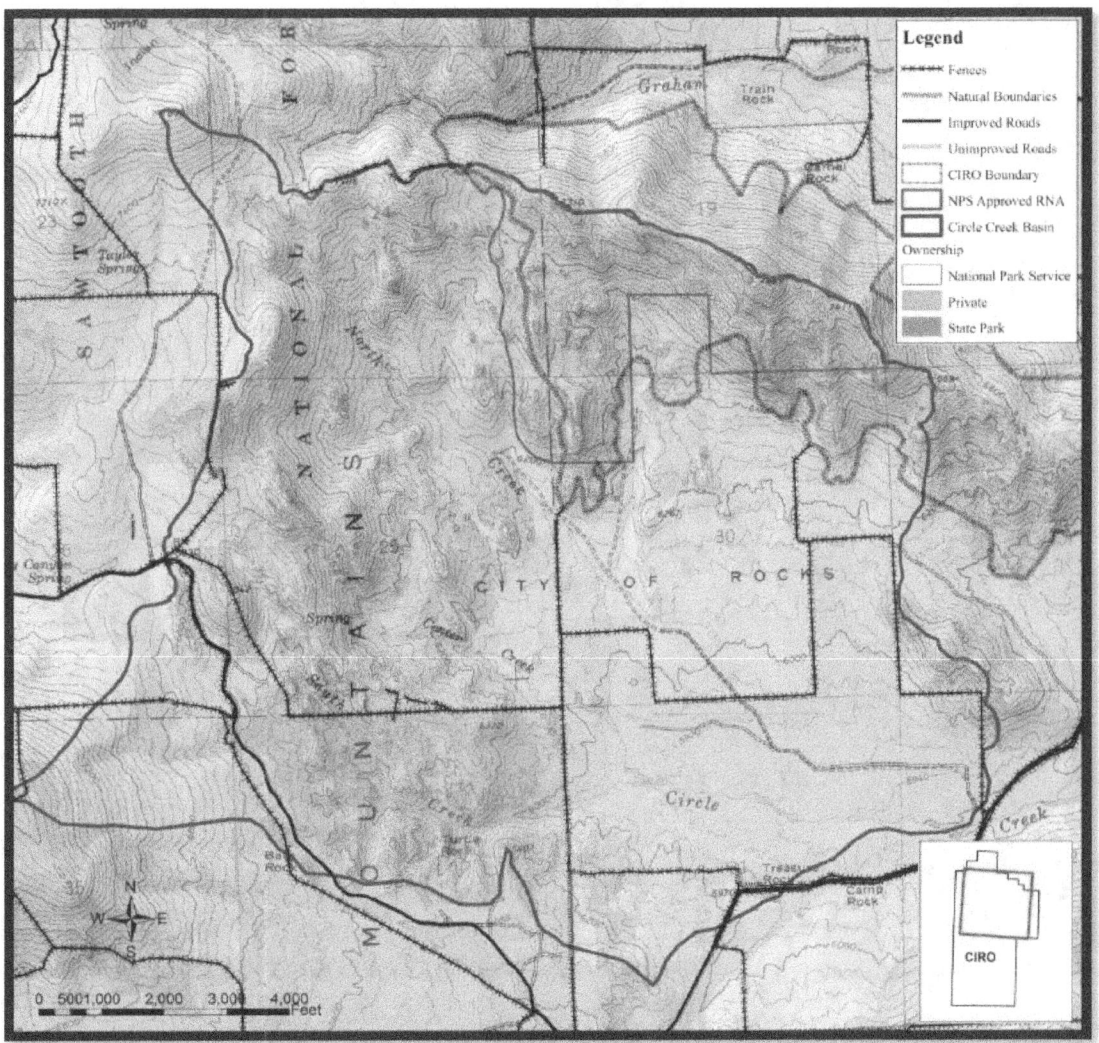

Figure 4. Map of Circle Creek basin in CIRO showing the location of the RNA, grazing allotments, and ownership.

Circle Creek basin is approximately 3,085 acres with the RNA occupying 10.1% of the area. The closest road to the RNA ends at the Circle Creek Overlook approximately ½ mile south of the southeast corner of the RNA. Circle Creek Overlook is the trailhead for several foot, horse, and mountain bike trails. A foot trail heads directly north to Steinfell's Dome climbing rock, which lies adjacent to the southeast corner of the RNA. The GeoWatt Trail (foot, horse, and bike approved) travels along the southern boundary and eventually ties in with the North Fork Circle Creek Trail (foot and horse approved) that lies west of the RNA (Figure 5).

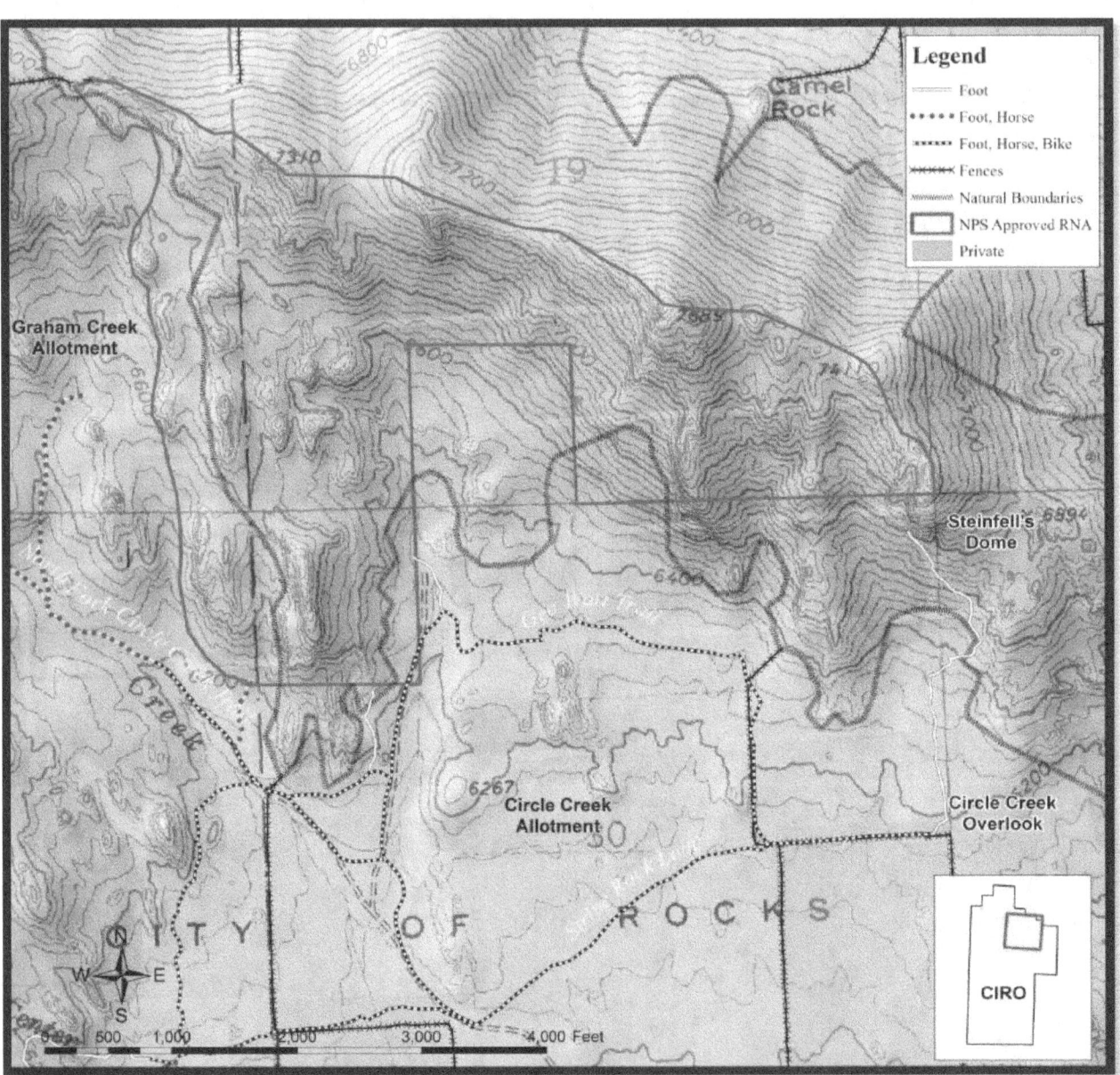

Figure 5. Map of trails surrounding the RNA.

Two grazing allotments surround the RNA. The Graham Creek allotment borders the RNA to the west and north (Figure 6). The boundary for this allotment intrudes into the west boundary of the RNA. The Circle Creek allotment lays to the south and east of the RNA with the allotment boundary intruding into the southern boundary in two locations (Figure 6). Both allotments are available for grazing from May 1st to September 30th under the current grazing management plans, but the actual turn-out and turn-off dates are established by the lessees and Superintendent (Sanders et.al. 1996).

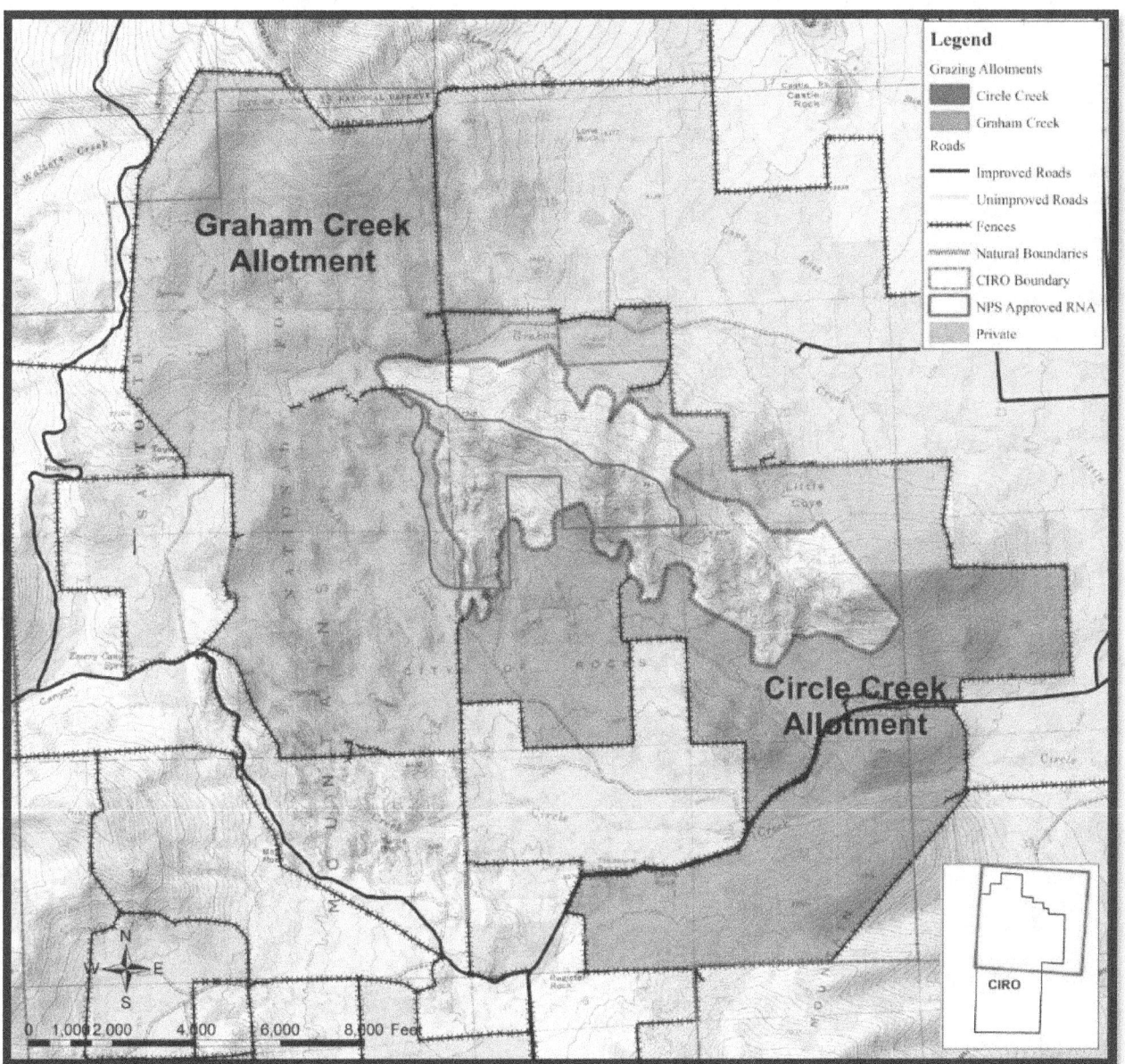

Figure 6. Map of CIRO grazing allotments surrounding the RNA.

Wildfires are a major natural process within the plant communities of CIRO. Morris (2006) found records for fourteen fires since 1926 totaling 14,320 acres. Only two of the fourteen fires were in or near the RNA. In 1977 the Pinion fire (45 acres) burned south of the RNA and entered the southwest corner of the unit (Figure 7). Eight years later in 1985 the Big Rock fire (60 acres) burned adjacent and west of the Pinion fire.

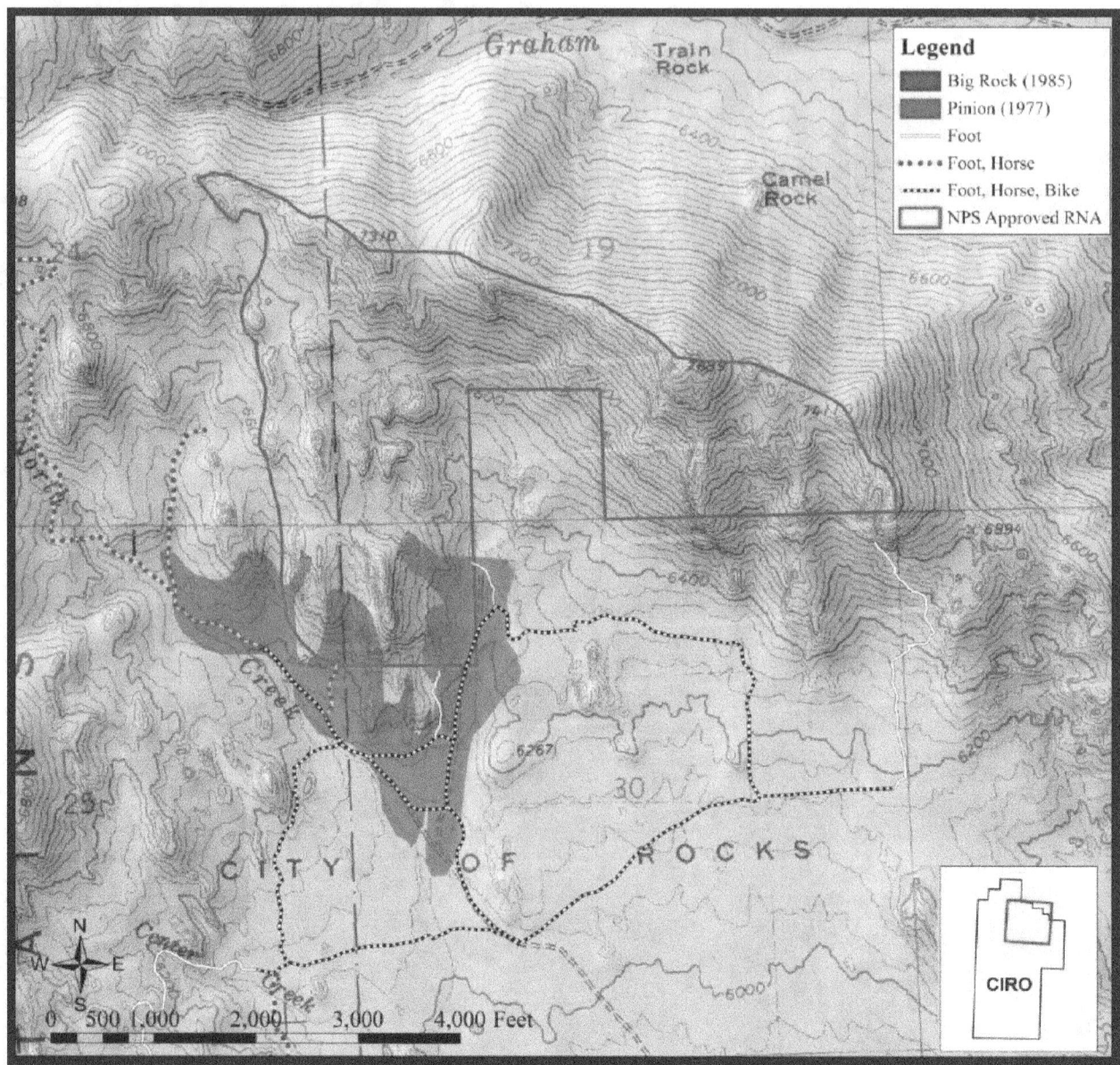

Figure 7. Past wildfires in and near the RNA.

The majority of the RNA consists of steep, forested slopes vegetated with various tree species. Singleleaf pinyon is the dominant tree species and occurs in mixed communities with Utah juniper and curl-leaf mountain mahogany (*Cercocarpus ledifolius*). These steep slopes rise to a ridge that borders the northern boundary of the RNA. Smaller portions of the RNA are more gently sloped shrub-grasslands with tree encroachment from the adjacent forest communities. There is a small unnamed drainage that flows into the North Fork Circle Creek that supports riparian habitat.

There are 531 species of plants (NPS 2005), 142 birds (NPS 2010 nb), 14 amphibians and reptiles (Shive and Peterson 2009), and 47 mammals (Rodhouse et.al. 2009) documented or expected in CIRO. The singleleaf pinyon/Utah juniper associations near cliffs and rock outcrops provides habitat for cliff chipmunks (*Tamias dorsalis*) and Piñon Mouse (*Peromyscus truei*) both classified as rare peripheral species of concern by Idaho Department of Fish and Game (IDFG). Rodhouse et. al. (2010) documented the importance of these associations in CIRO to both species along with other rodent species. Other fauna of note include mountain lion (*Felis concolor*), mule deer (*Odocoileus hemionus*), and elk (*Cervus canadensis*). The only sighting for ringtail cat (*Bassariscus astutus*) in Idaho was in CIRO but it is not considered a resident in Idaho by IDFG.

CIRO offers camping, climbing, hiking, backpacking, equestrian riding, mountain biking, sightseeing, and other recreational activities. About 80,000 visitors pass through CIRO annually, primarily from April 1 to October 30. Many come from the metropolitan areas of the Wasatch Front in Utah or the populated areas of southern Idaho (Boise, Twin Falls, Pocatello, and Idaho Falls). Nearly every state is represented in visitor registers and on camping receipts with Wyoming, California, Colorado, and Oregon most frequently listed. Visitors from up to twenty foreign countries are also represented annually. Although CIRO is open year-round, the roads are often impassable in winter.

Methods

GIS and Geodatabases

The majority of data used in this report is Geographical Information System (GIS) data in tabular form tied to spatial features, such as points, lines, and/or polygons. GIS software provides spatial analysis capabilities such as overlay, buffer, extraction, and modeling. Results are then displayed in map and tabular form. GIS software ARCMap Version 9.3 was used to store, edit, and display data.

A map project file (Figure 8) was developed for the CIRO RNA using ArcMap software that followed the behavioral rules for data in a single Microsoft Access database. Many types of geographic datasets can be collected within a map project file including feature classes, attribute tables, and raster data sets. The NPS ArcMap 8 1/2"x11" template was used in the map project files.

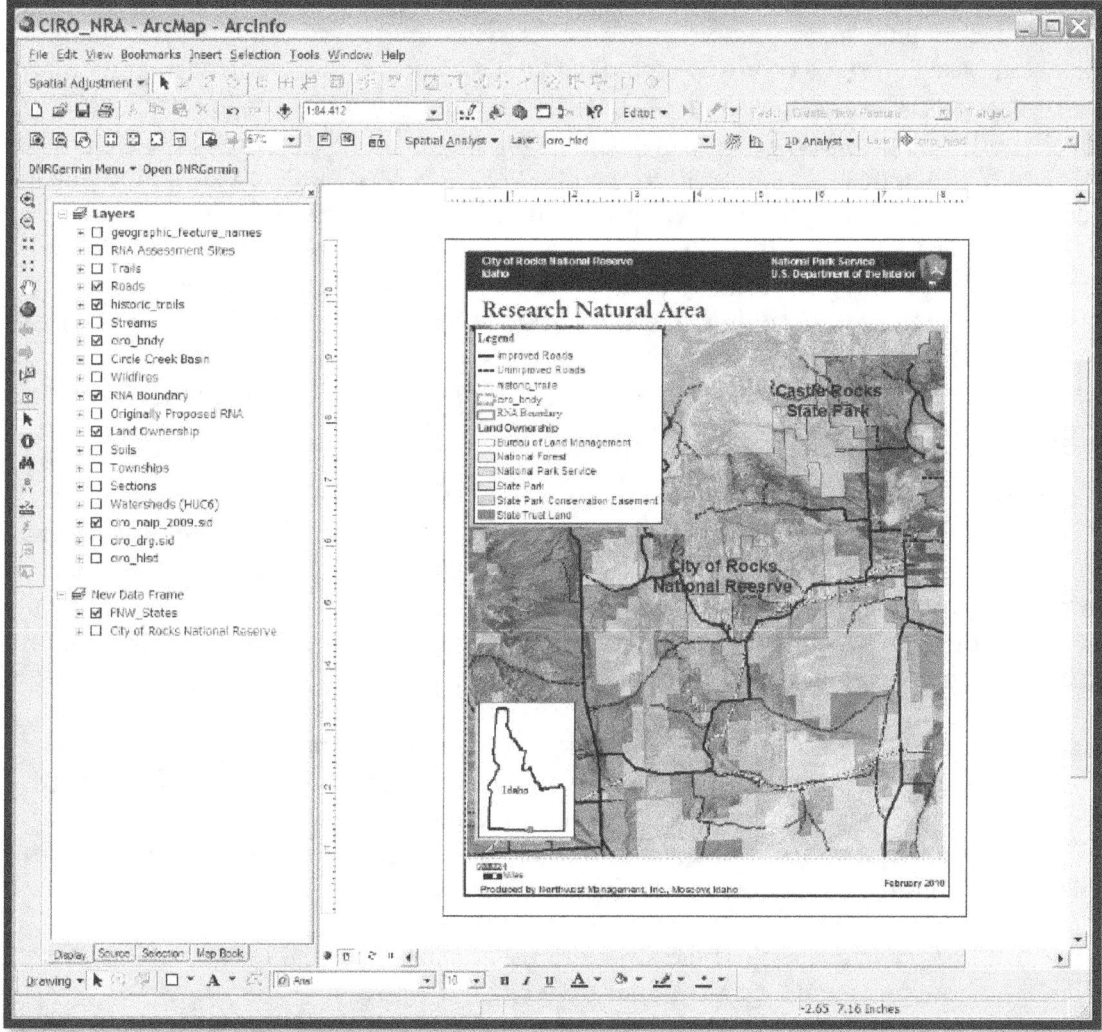

Figure 8. Screen capture of the CIRO RNA ArcGIS map project file.

13

The map project file was populated with GIS data through an extensive search of NPS sources and a multitude of local, state, and federal web sites. Data determined to be useful and accurate were re-projected into the North American Datum 1983 (NAD83) datum and the Universal Transverse Mercator (UTM) zone 12 projection. Metadata was generated for each layer in Federal Geographic Data Committee (FGDC) compliant format. Metadata describes the source, accuracy, data dictionary, projection, datum, and many other details about an individual layer.

All GIS data layers were imported into an ArcGIS File Geodatabase using ArcCatalog ver. 9.3 (ESRI 2006). Feature Data Sets were created based on theme type. A geodatabase is an ArcMap file structure that stores geometry, spatial reference system, attributed datasets, network datasets, topologies, and many other features. This GIS format provides a uniform method for storing and using GIS data and provides the flexibility to add new information as it becomes available.

Upland Assessment

A survey of the RNA was conducted the week of July 20 through July 24, 2009. A plant list was compiled along with some plant association notes. Particular attention was paid to searching for rare and endangered plants. Mammals, birds, and reptiles were recorded and various habitats were inspected based on signs or visual sightings. Human impacts were noted, in particular, evidence of grazing or mining. Given the significance of the singleleaf pinyon to the RNA, several of the larger trees were sized and aged. Twenty seven sample points in the RNA were recorded with photographs and the location recorded by GPS. A complete list of all plant species identified during the field inspection was developed. Vegetation maps are from a vegetation inventory project currently being conducted by Northwest Management, Inc., under contract with the Upper Columbia Basin Network. Vegetation plot data was collected in 2009 and photographic interpretation was completed from 2006 aerial photography. The map is considered to be in draft form prior to accuracy assessment in the summer of 2010. A Microsoft Access database was created to store all data and notes along with lookup tables and links to the 112 photographs taken in the RNA.

A rapid assessment method co-developed by the Natural Resources Conservation Service (NRCS), Agricultural Research Service (ARS), BLM, and the United States Geological Survey (USGS) was used to evaluate the health of two sites in the RNA. The method is described in the publication "Interpreting Indicators of Rangeland Health" (Pellant et al. 2005). The methodology is based on ecological sites; a land classification system based on the potential of land to produce distinctive kinds, amounts, and proportions of vegetation.

The rangeland health rapid assessment methodology is designed to provide a preliminary evaluation of 3 landscape attributes; soil stability, hydrologic function, and biologic integrity at the ecologic or site level. It was developed to assist land managers in identifying areas that are potentially at risk of degradation and assist in the selection of sites for developing monitoring programs. Definitions of these three closely interrelated attributes are:

> *Soil Stability*: The capacity of the site to limit redistribution and loss of soil resources including nutrients and organic matter by wind and water.

Hydrologic Function: The capacity of the site to capture, store, and safely release water from rainfall, run-on (inflow), and snowmelt (where relevant); to resist a reduction in this capacity; and to recover this capacity following degradation.

Biologic Integrity: The capacity of the site to support characteristic functional and structural communities in the context of normal variability, to resist loss of this function and structure due to disturbance, and to recover following disturbance.

This technique was developed as a tool for conducting moment-in-time qualitative assessments on rangeland status and as a communication and training tool for assisting land managers and other interested people to better understand rangeland ecological processes and their relationship to indicators (Pyke at. el. 2002) This method uses soil survey information, ecological site descriptions, and appropriate ecological reference areas to qualitatively assess rangeland health. As part of the assessment process, 17 indicators relating to these attributes are evaluated and the category descriptor or narrative that most closely describes the site is recorded. "Optional Indicators" may also be developed to meet local needs. The critical link between observations of indicators and determining the degree of departure from the ecological site description and/or ecological reference area is part of the interpretation process.

This technique does not provide for just one rating of rangeland health, but based upon a "preponderance of evidence" approach, it provides the departure from the ecological site description/ecological reference area(s) for the three attributes: soil stability, hydrologic function, and biologic integrity. There are 5 categories of departure recognized: "none to slight", "slight to moderate," "moderate," "moderate to extreme," and "extreme."

A slight modification of the methodology was implemented so multiple assessments in each ecological site could be combined for analysis. A rating from one (none to slight) to five (extreme) was assigned to each category. For ecological sites with more than one sample, an average was calculated for each indicator and then summed for each landscape attribute. There are ten indicators for soil stability and hydrologic function and nine for biologic integrity. The score for each landscape attribute was the sum of the indicators, minus the reference condition. Reference condition is based on a score of one for each indicator; equal to ten for soil stability and hydrologic function and nine for biologic integrity. Percent departure for each attribute was a proportion calculated by dividing the score by the maximum departure value; forty for soil stability and hydrologic function and thirty five for biologic integrity. The results are displayed graphically as a percent departure from the reference condition. For the narrative, the percent departure values are converted back into the associated qualitative categories: none to slight (<20%), slight to moderate (20-39%), moderate (40-59%), moderate to extreme (60-79%), and extreme ($\geq$80%).

All digital products for this report; including data, notes, and photographs; are on the DVD enclosed with the report located on the back cover.

Results

Upland Rapid Assessment

The entire RNA is classified and mapped as a Ola-rock outcrop-Earcree complex soils series (35%-55% slope). The Ola series occupies approximately 35% of the complex and is a coarse sandy loam up to 30" deep classified as a Loamy 16+ mountain sagebrush (*Artemisia tridentata* spp. *vaseyana*) /Idaho fescue (*Festuca idahoensis*) ecological site. This soil would occur on the lower slopes of the RNA on the south and west boundaries. The Earcree series makes up approximately 25% of the complex and is a gravelly coarse sandy loam up to 60" in depth. The two soils are intermixed with rock outcrops, which make up approximately 30% of the complex.

Two sample sites were selected in the Ola soil series located along the southern boundary where cattle grazing or other uses may have occurred in the past (Figure 9). Site 1 was on an 18% slope at 6,211' elevation and was dominated by mountain sagebrush (Figure 10). The site showed minor evidence of cattle grazing in the past and use by mule deer. Site 2 was on a steeper slope (58%) at 6,709' elevation and was also dominated by mountain sagebrush (Figure 11). The site had no evidence of cattle grazing and only minor use by mule deer. Both sites were rated as a none-slight departure from reference conditions for all 3 landscape attributes; soil stability (15%), hydrologic function (15%), and biologic integrity (10%). Both sites had minor amounts of cheatgrass (*Bromus tectorum*) and very few non-native forbs. These sites are in very good condition and are assumed to be functioning properly in all 3 major landscape processes. Individual landscape indicator values and the plant species lists with percent cover for each site are found in Appendix B and C, respectively.

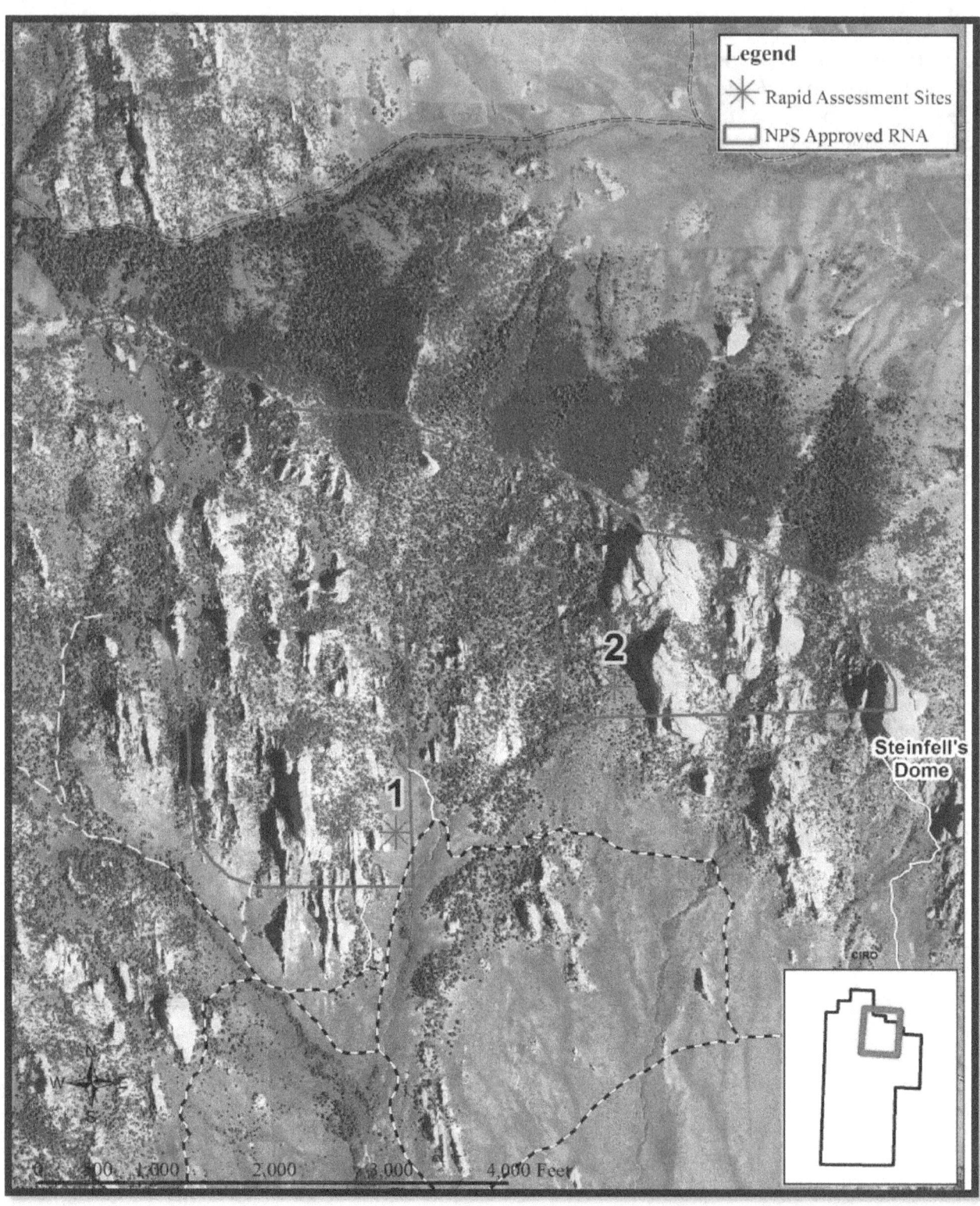

Figure 9. Map showing the location of the rapid assessment sites labeled by site number in the RNA.

Figure 10. Photographs of rapid assessment site 1 looking from plot center in the 4 cardinal directions.

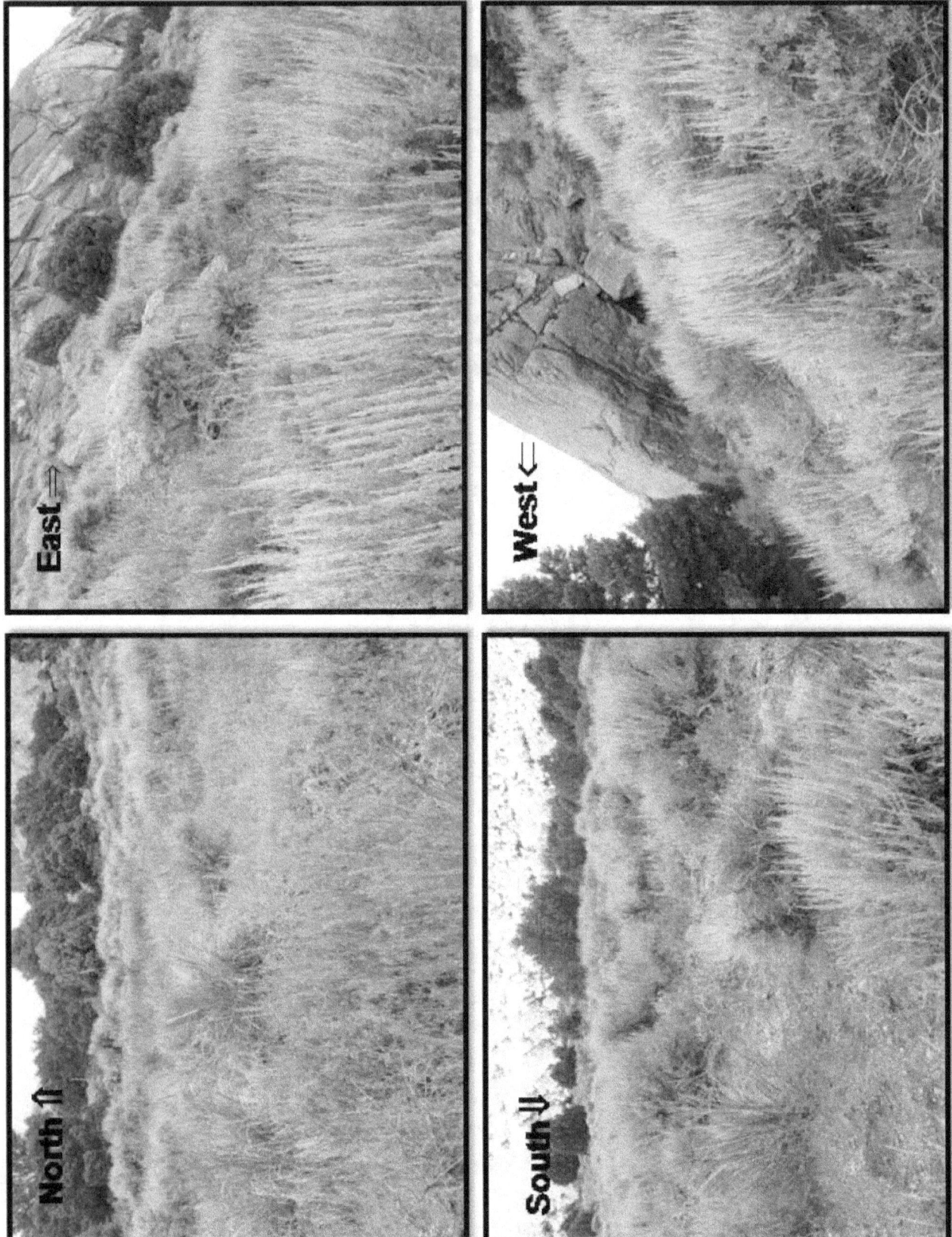

Figure 11. Photographs of rapid assessment site 2 looking from plot center in the 4 cardinal directions.

Vegetation

The spring of 2009 had above normal rainfall and the vegetation responded well to the increased moisture. Though the survey was late enough in the year to miss the earliest spring blooming plants, there was generally enough of the plant remaining for identification. A total of 211 taxa were recorded including varieties (Table 1). The list is not meant to be a complete vascular plant list for the RNA due to the limited time frame for inventory and the differential phenology of species preventing proper identification. No state or federally designated threatened or endangered plants were observed within the RNA during the survey. Davis' wavewing (*Cymopterus davisii*) is an Idaho endemic known to occur within CIRO on the eastern slopes of Graham Peak, in rock scree where late melting snows provide increased soil moisture during the growing season. Davis' wavewing was also considered a potential listed species in the RNA, but was not documented. One additional globally rare plant, Christ's paintbrush (*Castilleja christii*), an Idaho endemic, is found in the Albion range approximately 29 miles north on Mount Harrison at high elevations. Similar habitat occurs around Graham Peak within CIRO, but no plants have been found and appropriate habitat is not present within the RNA. Simpson's hedgehog cactus (*Pediocactus simpsonii*) is a CIRO special plant from the vegetation inventory project that is found throughout the park in dry open habitats and was observed at lower elevations of the RNA during the survey.

The condition of the vegetation is generally good with very few exotic plants. Of the 211 listed plant species 14 are listed as "Non-native." The most obvious and abundant non-native species are the annual grasses, Japanese brome (*Bromus japonicus*) and cheatgrass; as well as the perennial grass, bulbus bluegrass (*Poa bulbosa*). Tumble mustard (*Sisymbrium altissimum*) is widely scattered and not abundant. Other exotic annual forbs are commonly found, but rarely abundant.

Table 1. List of all plant species identified in the RNA during field survey from 7/20-24/2009.

Standard Scientific Name	Standard Common Name	Family	TSN	Nativity
Abies lasiocarpa	balsam fir, rocky mountain fir, subalpine fir, western balsam fir, white balsam	Pinaceae	181830	Native
Acer negundo	ashleaf maple, box elder, boxelder, boxelder maple, california boxelder, manitoba maple, western boxelder	Aceraceae	28749	Native
Achillea millefolium var. occidentalis	common yarrow, western yarrow	Asteraceae	526856	Native
Achnatherum hymenoides	Indian ricegrass	Poaceae	507943	Native
Achnatherum nelsonii	Columbia needlegrass, Nelson achnatherum	Poaceae	507948	Native
Achnatherum nevadense	Nevada needlegrass	Poaceae	507949	Native
Agastache urticifolia	horsemint giant hyssop, nettleleaf giant hyssop	Lamiaceae	32450	Native

Table 1. List of all plant species identified in the RNA during field survey from 7/20-24/2009 (continued).

Standard Scientific Name	Standard Common Name	Family	TSN	Nativity
Agoseris glauca var. glauca	pale agoseris	Asteraceae	182407	Native
Agoseris heterophylla	annual agoseris, annual goatsbeard, mountain dandelion	Asteraceae	36492	Native
Agropyron desertorum	clustered wheat grass, desert wheatgrass	Poaceae	40372	Non-Native
Agrostis scabra	rough bent, rough bentgrass, ticklegrass	Poaceae	40424	Native
Agrostis stolonifera	carpet bentgrass, creeping bent, creeping bentgrass, redtop, redtop bent, seaside bentgrass, spreading bent	Poaceae	40400	Native
Allium acuminatum	taper-tip onion, tapertip onion	Liliaceae	42707	Native
Alyssum desertorum	desert alyssum, desert madwort	Brassicaceae	23032	Non-Native
Amelanchier alnifolia	Saskatoon serviceberry, juneberry, pacific serviceberry, western serviceberry, western shadbush	Rosaceae	25109	Native
Antennaria dimorpha	low everlasting, low pussytoes	Asteraceae	36727	Native
Antennaria microphylla	Rocky Mountain pussytoes, littleleaf pussytoes, small leaf everlasting, smallleaf pussytoes	Asteraceae	185162	Native
Aquilegia formosa	crimson columbine, western columbine	Ranunculaceae	18738	Native
Arabis glabra	tower rockcress, tower-mustard	Brassicaceae	22695	Native
Arabis hirsuta	hairy rockcress	Brassicaceae	184344	Native
Arabis holboellii var. retrofracta	a holboell rock-cress, second rockcress	Brassicaceae	184362	Native
Arabis lignifera	desert rockcress, woody rockcress	Brassicaceae	22708	Native
Arabis microphylla	littleleaf rockcress, small leaf rockcress	Brassicaceae	22711	Native
Arabis sparsiflora	fewleaf rockcress, sicklepod rockcress	Brassicaceae	22735	Native
Arnica sororia	twin arnica	Asteraceae	36576	Native
Artemisia dracunculus	false tarragon, green sagewort, silky wormwood, tarragon, wormwood	Asteraceae	35462	Native
Artemisia ludoviciana var. incompta	No data	Asteraceae	532350	Native
Artemisia ludoviciana var. latifolia	No data	Asteraceae	532351	Native
Artemisia ludoviciana var. ludoviciana	No data	Asteraceae	-501970	Native

Table 1. List of all plant species identified in the RNA during field survey from 7/20-24/2009 (continued).

Standard Scientific Name	Standard Common Name	Family	TSN	Nativity
Artemisia tridentata ssp. vaseyana	big sagebrush, mountain big sagebrush	Asteraceae	183740	Native
Astragalus cibarius	browse milkvetch	Fabaceae	25463	Native
Astragalus lentiginosus var. salinus	salty loco milkvetch	Fabaceae	192584	Native
Astragalus purshii var. purshii	Pursh's milk-vetch, Pursh's milkvetch, woollypod milkvetch	Fabaceae	192724	Native
Balsamorhiza sagittata	arrowleaf balsamroot	Asteraceae	36818	Native
Brickellia californica	California brickellbush	Asteraceae	36866	Native
Brickellia grandiflora	mountain brickellbush, tasselflower brickellbush, tasselflower brickellia	Asteraceae	36878	Native
Bromus carinatus	California brome, mountain brome	Poaceae	40481	Native
Bromus japonicus	Japanese brome, Japanese bromegrass, Japanese chess	Poaceae	40479	Non-Native
Bromus tectorum	cheat grass, cheatgrass, downy brome, early chess, military grass, wild oats	Poaceae	40524	Non-Native
Calochortus nuttallii	sego lily, sego-lily	Liliaceae	42863	Native
Camelina microcarpa	false flax, little-pod false flax, littlepod false flax, littlepod falseflax, littleseed falseflax, small fruited falseflax, smallseed falseflax	Brassicaceae	22599	Non-Native
Camissonia subacaulis	diffuseflower evening-primrose, longleaf suncup, northern eveningprimrose	Onagraceae	27555	Native
Capsella bursa-pastoris	shepardspurse, shepherd's purse, shepherd's-purse, shepherdspurse	Brassicaceae	22766	Non-Native
Carex hoodii	Hood's sedge, hood sedge	Cyperaceae	39642	Native
Carex microptera	ovalhead sedge, smallwing sedge	Cyperaceae	39699	Native
Carex nebrascensis	Nebraska sedge	Cyperaceae	39711	Native
Carex petasata	Liddon sedge, Liddon's sedge	Cyperaceae	39751	Native
Carex praegracilis	clustered field sedge, slim sedge	Cyperaceae	39767	Native
Carex rossii	Ross sedge, Ross' sedge, Ross's sedge, shortstemmed sedge	Cyperaceae	39786	Native
Castilleja flava	yellow Indian paintbrush, yellow paintbrush	Scrophulariaceae	33115	Native
Castilleja linariifolia	Wyoming Indian paintbrush, Wyoming paintbrush	Scrophulariaceae	33138	Native

Table 1. List of all plant species identified in the RNA during field survey from 7/20-24/2009 (continued).

Standard Scientific Name	Standard Common Name	Family	TSN	Nativity
Cerastium nutans	common chickweed, longstem chickweed, nodding chickweed, nodding mouse-ear chickweed	Caryophyllaceae	19958	Native
Cercocarpus ledifolius	curl-leaf mountain mahogany, curlleaf cercocarpus, curlleaf mountain mahogany, curlleaf mountainmahogany	Rosaceae	25134	Native
Chaenactis douglasii	Douglas dustymaiden, Douglas' dustymaiden, Douglas' pincushion, dusty maiden, dusty-maiden	Asteraceae	36987	Native
Chenopodium album	common lambsquarters, lambsquarters, lambsquarters goosefoot, white goosefoot	Chenopodiaceae	20592	Non-Native
Chenopodium glaucum	oak-leaf goosefoot, oakleaf goosefoot	Chenopodiaceae	20610	Native
Chrysothamnus nauseosus ssp. albicaulis	No data	Asteraceae	37056	Native
Chrysothamnus nauseosus ssp. consimilis	No data	Asteraceae	37061	Native
Chrysothamnus viscidiflorus ssp. lanceolatus	lanceleaf low rabbitbrush, lanceleaf rabbitbrush, yellow rabbitbrush	Asteraceae	37094	Native
Chrysothamnus viscidiflorus ssp. puberulus	downy rabbitbrush, hairy low rabbitbrush, yellow rabbitbrush	Asteraceae	37093	Native
Cirsium neomexicanum var. utahense	Utah thistle	Asteraceae	527375	Native
Cirsium undulatum	gray thistle, wavy-leaf thistle, wavyleaf thistle	Asteraceae	36423	Non-Native
Cirsium vulgare	bull thistle, common thistle, spear thistle	Asteraceae	36428	Non-Native
Claytonia perfoliata	miner's lettuce, miners lettuce, minerslettuce	Portulacaceae	20395	Native
Clematis ligusticifolia	virgin'sbower, virgins bower, virginsbower, western white clematis	Ranunculaceae	18702	Native
Collinsia parviflora	blue-eyed Mary, littleflower collinsia, maiden blue eyed Mary, small-flower blue-eyed mary, smallflower blue eyed Mary	Scrophulariaceae	33534	Native
Collomia linearis	narrow-leaf mountain-trumpet, narrowleaf mountaintrumpet, slenderleaf collomia, tiny trumpet	Polemoniaceae	31041	Native
Comandra umbellata var. pallida	No data	Santalaceae	533741	Native
Crepis acuminata	long-leaf hawksbeard, longleaf hawksbeard, tapertip hawksbeard	Asteraceae	37169	Native
Cryptantha ambigua	Wickes cryptantha, Wilkes cryptantha, basin cryptantha	Boraginaceae	31783	Native

Table 1. List of all plant species identified in the RNA during field survey from 7/20-24/2009 (continued).

Standard Scientific Name	Standard Common Name	Family	TSN	Nativity
Cryptantha humilis	round-spike catseye, roundspike cryptantha	Boraginaceae	31820	Native
Cryptantha watsonii	Watson cryptantha, Watson's cryptantha	Boraginaceae	31780	Native
Cystopteris fragilis	brittle bladder fern, brittle bladderfern, fragile fern	Dryopteridaceae	17482	Native
Danthonia unispicata	onespike danthonia, onespike oatgrass	Poaceae	41636	Native
Delphinium depauperatum	slim larkspur, wand larkspur	Ranunculaceae	18552	Native
Delphinium nuttallianum	Nuttal's larkspur, Nuttall larkspur, Nuttall's larkspur, low larkspur, two-lobe larkspur, twolobe larkspur	Ranunculaceae	18483	Native
Deschampsia danthonioides	annual hairgrass	Poaceae	40593	Native
Descurainia californica	Sierra tansymustard, Sierran tansy mustard, Sierran tansymustard	Brassicaceae	22821	Native
Descurainia richardsonii var. brevipes	No data	Brassicaceae	534399	Native
Dodecatheon pulchellum	Southern shootingstar, dark-throat shootingstar, darkthroat shootingstar	Primulaceae	23945	Native
Draba nemorosa	wood draba, woodland Whitlow-grass, woodland draba, woods draba	Brassicaceae	22894	Native
Draba verna	spring Whitlowgrass, spring draba	Brassicaceae	22923	Native
Eleocharis quinqueflora	few-flower spike-rush, few-flower spikerush, fewflower spikerush, fewflowered spikesedge	Cyperaceae	502240	Native
Elymus elymoides var. elymoides	No data	Poaceae	-502289	Native
Elymus glaucus	blue wild rye, blue wildrye	Poaceae	40684	Native
Elymus lanceolatus	streambank wheatgrass, streamside wild rye	Poaceae	502267	Native
Elymus trachycaulus var. trachycaulus	No data	Poaceae	-502295	Native
Epilobium brachycarpum	autumn willowherb, autumn willowweed, tall annual willowherb	Onagraceae	27288	Native
Ericameria nana	dwarf goldenbush, low goldenbush	Asteraceae	502366	Native
Erigeron compositus var. glabratus	No data	Asteraceae	535024	Native
Erigeron divergens	spreading daisy, spreading fleabane	Asteraceae	35852	Native
Erigeron pumilus ssp. concinnoides var. condensatus	No data	Asteraceae	-502326	Native
Eriogonum heracleoides	Wyeth eriogonum, Wyeth's buckwheat, parsnipflower buckwheat	Polygonaceae	21150	Native

Table 1. List of all plant species identified in the RNA during field survey from 7/20-24/2009 (continued).

Standard Scientific Name	Standard Common Name	Family	TSN	Nativity
Eriogonum microthecum var. laxiflorum	slender buckwheat	Polygonaceae	528009	Native
Eriogonum umbellatum	sulfer flower buckwheat, sulfur buckwheat, sulfur eriogonum, sulphur wildbuckwheat, sulphur-flower buckwheat	Polygonaceae	21266	Native
Erysimum asperum	No data	Brassicaceae	22931	Native
Eucephalus elegans	elegant aster	Asteraceae	513251	Native
Festuca idahoensis	Idaho fescue	Poaceae	40816	Native
Fritillaria atropurpurea	leopard lily, spotted fritillary, spotted missionbells	Liliaceae	502669	Native
Fritillaria pudica	yellow bells, yellow fritillary, yellow missionbells, yellowbells	Liliaceae	42936	Native
Galium aparine	bedstraw, catchweed bedstraw, cleavers, cleaverwort, goose grass, scarthgrass, sticky-willy, stickywilly, white hedge	Rubiaceae	34797	Native
Galium triflorum	fragrant bedstraw, sweet bedstraw, sweetscented bedstraw	Rubiaceae	34933	Native
Gayophytum diffusum	bigflower groundsmoke, spreading groundsmoke	Onagraceae	27671	Native
Gayophytum ramosissimum	muchbranched groundsmoke, pinyon groundsmoke	Onagraceae	27679	Native
Geranium viscosissimum var. incisum	sticky purple geranium	Geraniaceae	566245	Native
Gilia tenerrima	delicate gilia	Polemoniaceae	31181	Native
Grindelia squarrosa var. serrulata	curly-cup gumweed, curlycup gumweed, curlytop gumweed, gumweed, rosinweed, tarweed	Asteraceae	528288	Native
Hackelia patens	common stickseed, spotted stickseed	Boraginaceae	31916	Native
Haplopappus acaulis	No data	Asteraceae	37499	Native
Helianthella uniflora	oneflower helianthella	Asteraceae	37598	Native
Helianthus nuttallii	Nuttall sunflower, Nuttall's sunflower	Asteraceae	36662	Native
Hesperostipa comata var. comata	No data	Poaceae	-502432	Native
Heterotheca villosa	hairy false goldaster, hairy false goldenaster, hairy goldaster, hairy goldenaster	Asteraceae	37689	Native
Heuchera cylindrica var. alpina	alpine alumroot	Saxifragaceae	528403	Native

Table 1. List of all plant species identified in the RNA during field survey from 7/20-24/2009 (continued).

Standard Scientific Name	Standard Common Name	Family	TSN	Nativity
Heuchera parvifolia var. utahensis	Utah alumroot	Saxifragaceae	528425	Native
Heuchera rubescens	pink alumroot	Saxifragaceae	24373	Native
Holodiscus dumosus	bush oceanspray, rockspirea	Rosaceae	25178	Native
Hydrophyllum capitatum var. alpinum	alpine waterleaf	Hydrophyllaceae	528507	Native
Ionactis alpina	Lava aster, crag aster	Asteraceae	507020	Native
Iris missouriensis	Rocky Mountain iris, western blue flag, wild iris, wildiris	Iridaceae	43221	Native
Juncus balticus var. montanus	mountain rush	Juncaceae	528598	Native
Juncus bufonius	toad rush	Juncaceae	39227	Native
Juncus confusus	Colorado rush	Juncaceae	39261	Native
Juniperus osteosperma	Utah juniper	Cupressaceae	194859	Native
Juniperus scopulorum	Rocky Mountain juniper	Cupressaceae	194872	Native
Koeleria macrantha	junegrass, prairie Junegrass	Poaceae	503284	Native
Lactuca serriola	China lettuce, prickly lettuce, wild lettuce	Asteraceae	36608	Non-Native
Lappula redowskii	No data	Boraginaceae	32046	Native
Leptodactylon pungens	common pricklygilia, granite gilia, granite prickly gilia, granite prickly phlox, granite pricklygilia	Polemoniaceae	31233	Native
Leucopoa kingii	spike fescue, spike-fescue	Poaceae	41832	Native
Leymus cinereus	basin wildrye	Poaceae	503433	Native
Linum lewisii	Lewis blue flax, Lewis flax, Lewis' flax, blue flax, prairie flax	Linaceae	29214	Native
Lithophragma glabrum	bulbous woodland-star, bulbous woodlandstar, smooth woodlandstar	Saxifragaceae	24395	Native
Lithophragma parviflorum	smallflower woodland-star, smallflower woodlandstar	Saxifragaceae	24398	Native
Lithospermum ruderale	western gromwell, western stoneseed, white stoneseed	Boraginaceae	31953	Native
Lomatium foeniculaceum var. macdougalii	No data	Apiaceae	536921	Native
Lomatium triternatum var. platycarpum	No data	Apiaceae	-502540	Native
Lupinus argenteus var. argentatus	No data	Fabaceae	566449	Native

Table 1. List of all plant species identified in the RNA during field survey from 7/20-24/2009 (continued).

Standard Scientific Name	Standard Common Name	Family	TSN	Nativity
Lupinus leucophyllus	velvet lupine, whiteleaf lupine	Fabaceae	26049	Native
Machaeranthera canescens	hoary aster, hoary goldenweed, hoary machaeranthera, hoary tansy-aster, hoary tansyaster, purple aster	Asteraceae	37984	Native
Madia gracilis	grassy tarweed, slender tarweed	Asteraceae	38030	Native
Mahonia repens	Oregongrape, creeping barberry, creeping mahonia, oregon grape, trunkee barberry	Berberidaceae	195045	Native
Maianthemum stellatum	Starry false solomon's-seal, false Solomons seal, starry Solomon's-seal, starry false Solomon's seal, starry false lily of the valley	Liliaceae	503656	Native
Melica bulbosa	bulbous oniongrass, oniongrass	Poaceae	41851	Native
Mentzelia albicaulis	white blazingstar, whitestem blazingstar, whitestem stickleaf	Loasaceae	503757	Native
Mertensia oblongifolia	languid-lady, oblongleaf bluebells	Boraginaceae	31683	Native
Microseris nutans	nodding microceris, nodding silverpuffs	Asteraceae	38114	Native
Microsteris gracilis var. humilior	No data	Polemoniaceae	537538	Native
Mimulus guttatus	common monkeyflower, seep monkeyflower	Scrophulariaceae	33236	Native
Muhlenbergia richardsonis	mat muhly, soft-leaf muhly	Poaceae	41938	Native
Myosotis stricta	strict forget me not, strict forget-me-not	Boraginaceae	503897	Non-Native
Nemophila breviflora	Great Basin blue-eyes, baby blueeyes, basin nemophila	Hydrophyllaceae	31423	Native
Opuntia polyacantha	plains pricklypear	Cactaceae	19726	Native
Orobanche fasciculata	clustered broom-rape	Orobanchaceae	34290	Native
Osmorhiza occidentalis	sweetanise, western sweetroot	Apiaceae	29792	Native
Packera cana	woolly groundsel	Asteraceae	518142	Native
Packera multilobata	lobeleaf groundsel	Asteraceae	518150	Native
Packera streptanthifolia	Rocky Mountain groundsel	Asteraceae	518158	Native
Penstemon attenuatus var. militaris	South Idaho penstemon	Scrophulariaceae	529464	Native
Penstemon cyananthus var. subglaber	Wasatch beardtongue	Scrophulariaceae	529469	Native
Perideridia montana	No data	Apiaceae	518708	Native

Table 1. List of all plant species identified in the RNA during field survey from 7/20-24/2009 (continued).

Standard Scientific Name	Standard Common Name	Family	TSN	Nativity
Phacelia hastata	silver-leaf scorpion-weed, silverleaf phacelia, spearhead phacelia	Hydrophyllaceae	31529	Native
Phlox hoodii var. canescens	No data	Polemoniaceae	538685	Native
Pinus contorta var. latifolia	lodgepole pine, tall lodgepole pine	Pinaceae	529673	Native
Pinus flexilis	limber pine, rocky mountain white pine	Pinaceae	183343	Native
Pinus monophylla	nut pine, one-leaf pine, singleleaf pinyon	Pinaceae	183353	Native
Plectritis macrocera	longhorn plectritis, white cornsalad	Valerianaceae	35383	Native
Poa bulbosa	bulbous blue grass, bulbous bluegrass	Poaceae	41116	Native
Poa pratensis	Kentucky bluegrass	Poaceae	41088	Native
Poa secunda	Sandberg bluegrass, Sandberg's bluegrass, big bluegrass	Poaceae	41103	Native
Polygonum douglasii var. douglasii	No data	Polygonaceae	-502745	Native
Populus tremuloides	quaking aspen	Salicaceae	195773	Native
Potentilla arguta	tall cinquefoil	Rosaceae	24692	Native
Potentilla glandulosa var. intermedia	No data	Rosaceae	539206	Native
Potentilla gracilis var. pulcherrima	No data	Rosaceae	539216	Native
Prunus virginiana var. melanocarpa	black chokecherry, choke cherry	Rosaceae	529894	Native
Pseudoroegneria spicata	bluebunch wheatgrass, bluebunch-wheat grass	Poaceae	504637	Native
Pseudotsuga menziesii var. glauca	Douglas fir, Rocky Mountain Douglas-fir, blue douglas fir, colorado douglas fir, inland douglas fir, rocky mountain douglas fir	Pinaceae	183428	Native
Purshia tridentata	antelope bitterbrush	Rosaceae	25290	Native
Ranunculus andersonii	Anderson's buttercup, pink buttercup	Ranunculaceae	18590	Native
Ribes cereum var. pedicellare	squaw currant, whisky currant, white squaw currant	Grossulariaceae	530048	Native
Rosa woodsii var. ultramontana	Woods' rose	Rosaceae	530129	Native
Rumex crispus	Curley dock, curly dock, narrowleaf dock, sour dock, yellow dock	Polygonaceae	20937	Native
Salix geyeriana	Geyer willow, Geyer's willow	Salicaceae	504965	Native
Salix scouleriana	Scouler willow, Scouler's willow	Salicaceae	504980	Native

Table 1. List of all plant species identified in the RNA during field survey from 7/20-24/2009 (continued).

Standard Scientific Name	Standard Common Name	Family	TSN	Nativity
Schoenocrambe linifolia	flaxleaf plainsmustard, rush mustard	Brassicaceae	23296	Native
Sedum lanceolatum	lance-leaf stonecrop, lanceleaf stonecrop, spearleaf stonecrop	Crassulaceae	24126	Native
Senecio integerrimus var. exaltatus	Columbia groundsel, Columbia ragwort	Asteraceae	530318	Native
Silene douglasii	Douglas' campion, seabluff catchfly	Caryophyllaceae	20065	Native
Silene menziesii var. menziesii	Menzies' campion	Caryophyllaceae	566803	Native
Sisymbrium altissimum	Jim Hill mustard, tall hedge-mustard, tall mustard, tall tumblemustard, tumble mustard, tumblemustard, tumbleweed mustard	Brassicaceae	23312	Non-Native
Smilacina racemosa	No data	Liliaceae	43036	Native
Solidago canadensis	Canada goldenrod, Canadian goldenrod, common goldenrod	Asteraceae	36224	Native
Solidago missouriensis	Missouri goldenrod, prairie goldenrod	Asteraceae	36277	Native
Stellaria longipes	long-stalk starwort, longstalk starwort	Caryophyllaceae	20168	Native
Stephanomeria minor var. myrioclada	narrowleaf wirelettuce	Asteraceae	566324	Native
Stipa comata var. comata	needleandthread	Poaceae	530571	Native
Symphoricarpos oreophilus	mountain snowberry, whortleleaf snowberry	Caprifoliaceae	35338	Native
Symphyotrichum ascendens	western aster	Asteraceae	522184	Native
Taraxacum officinale	blowball, common dandelion, dandelion, faceclock	Asteraceae	36213	Native
Tetradymia canescens	gray horsebrush, spineless horsebrush	Asteraceae	38494	Native
Tragopogon dubius	Western goat's beard, common salsify, goat's beard, goatsbeard, meadow goat's-beard, salsifis majeur, salsify, western salsify, wild oysterplant, yellow goat's beard, yellow salsify	Asteraceae	38564	Non-Native
Trifolium cyathiferum	cup clover	Fabaceae	26235	Native
Trifolium microcephalum	littlehead clover, small-head clover, smallhead clover	Fabaceae	26286	Native
Verbascum thapsus	big taper, common mullein, flannel mullein, flannel plant, great mullein, mullein, velvet dock, velvet plant, woolly mullein	Scrophulariaceae	33394	Non-Native
Viola purpurea	goose-foot yellow violet, goosefoot violet, pine violet	Violaceae	22145	Native

Table 1. List of all plant species identified in the RNA during field survey from 7/20-24/2009 (continued).

Standard Scientific Name	Standard Common Name	Family	TSN	Nativity
Viola vallicola var. vallicola	sagebrush violet	Violaceae	530843	Native
Vulpia octoflora	eight-flower six-weeks grass, pullout grass, sixweeks fescue, sixweeks grass	Poaceae	42264	Native
Zigadenus paniculatus	foothill deathcamas, sand-corn	Liliaceae	43167	Native

Several areas in the RNA are shrub-dominated with mountain sagebrush the most common. It is mixed with other shrubs such as bitterbrush (*Purshia tridentata*), mountain snowberry (*Symphoricarpos oreophilus*), and various graminodes such as needle and thread grass (*Hesperostipa comata*), desert wheatgrass (*Agropyron desertorum*), Sandberg's bluegrass (*Poa secunda*), and streambank wheatgrass (*Elymus lanceolatus*). These observations agree with the plant communities listed for the proposed RNA in CIRO by Wellner and Johnson (1984) in their letter to the BLM State Director, Clair N. Whitlock, dated February 28, 1984. The table attached to the letter listed the following plant communities:

- *Artemisia tridentata* ssp. *vaseyana/Festuca idahoensis*
- *Artemisia tridentata* ssp. *vaseyana-Symphoricarpos oreophilus/Festuca idahoensis*
- *Cercocarpus ledifolius/Symphoricarpos oreophilus*
- *Pinus monophylla-Juniperus osteosperma/Prunus virginianus*
- *Pinus monophylla-Juniperus osteosperma/Elymus cinereus*
- *Pinus monophylla-Juniperus osteosperma/Cercocarpus ledifolius*

The observations of Wellner and Johnson (1984) concur with the vegetation map of CIRO. The draft vegetation map for CIRO was completed at the plant associations/alliances level. Table 2 is a summary of the plant associations/alliances found in the RNA. Singleleaf pinyon–Utah juniper classes (two map classes) make up 36.7% of the RNA. Bare ground/rocks accounts for 25.1% of the area and is spatial intermixed with the vegetation classes (Figure 12).

Table 2. Vegetation classes mapped from the vegetation inventory project in the RNA.

Class Description	# Polygons	Acres	% Area
Pinus flexilis Woodland Alliance	3	23.8	7.6%
Pinus monophylla - Juniperus spp./ (Purshia tridentata) Artemisia spp. Woodland Complex	3	8.2	2.6%
Pinus monophylla - (Juniperus osteosperma) / Cercocarpus ledifolius Woodland	9	107.4	34.1%
Populus tremuloides Dry Herbaceous Woodland Complex	2	3.3	1.1%
Populus tremuloides - Juniperus scopulorum Woodland	9	28.3	9.0%
Cercocarpus ledifolius / Symphoricarpos oreophilus Woodland	11	47.4	15.1%
Artemisia tridentata ssp. tridentata Shrubland Alliance	1	0.1	0.0%
Artemisia tridentata ssp. vaseyana - Symphoricarpos oreophilus Shrubland	5	6.9	2.2%
Artemisia tridentata vaseyana / Mixed Herbaceous Shrubland Complex	3	10.4	3.3%
Bare Rock / Sand / Other Bare Ground	53	79.1	25.1%

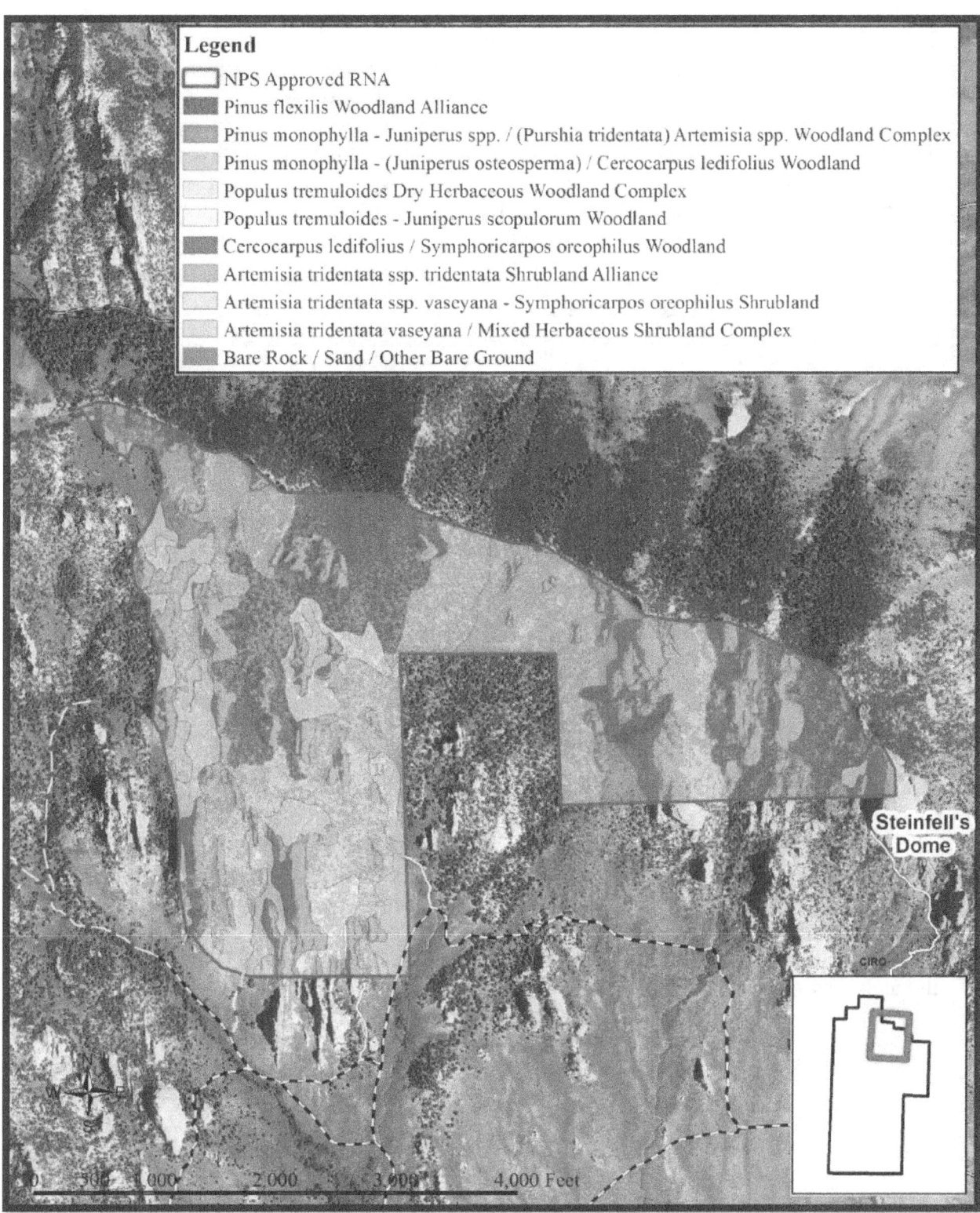

Legend

☐ NPS Approved RNA
▓ Pinus flexilis Woodland Alliance
▓ Pinus monophylla - Juniperus spp. / (Purshia tridentata) Artemisia spp. Woodland Complex
▓ Pinus monophylla - (Juniperus osteosperma) / Cercocarpus ledifolius Woodland
☐ Populus tremuloides Dry Herbaceous Woodland Complex
☐ Populus tremuloides - Juniperus scopulorum Woodland
▓ Cercocarpus ledifolius / Symphoricarpos orcophilus Woodland
▓ Artemisia tridentata ssp. tridentata Shrubland Alliance
☐ Artemisia tridentata ssp. vaseyana - Symphoricarpos orcophilus Shrubland
☐ Artemisia tridentata vaseyana / Mixed Herbaceous Shrubland Complex
▓ Bare Rock / Sand / Other Bare Ground

Steinfell's Dome

Figure 12. Map of vegetation classes in the RNA based on vegetation inventory project.

33

Singleleaf pinyon is the most common tree species in the RNA and is reproducing well, as evidenced by many seedling and sapling trees. The larger trees in the RNA, singleleaf pinyon and limber pine, were measured to determine size and age. The measured trees were 20-30" diameter at breast height (dbh) and 35-50' tall (Table 3 and Figure 13). The largest tree measured was 34.5" dbh and 54' tall. The trees in the RNA are taller and older than the average for singleleaf pinyon across the range of the specie, which maybe the result of favorable growing conditions and lack of recent wildfire (Figure 14). Singleleaf pinyon is a long lived tree, reaching maximum seed production at about 160-200 years old and is known to live up to 800-1000 years (Christopher 2008).

Table 3. List of measured trees in the RNA with diameter, height, and age.

Site No.	Species	Diameter	Height	Age (years)	Elevation	Slope	Aspect
3	*Pinus monophylla*	19.6"	39'		6386	50	E
4	*Pinus monophylla*	27.6"	63'	320	6474	40	NE
8	*Pinus monophylla*	25.2"	50'	315	6639	50	NNE
12	*Pinus flexilis*	31.1"	65'	314	6884	40	SE
17	*Pinus flexilis*	23.2"	57'		6734	40	E
20	*Pinus monophylla*	34.5"	54'	410	6482	50	E
20	*Pinus monophylla*	23.2"	42'	310	6482	50	E

The second most abundant forest component of the RNA is curl-leaf mountain mahogany. This species of tree is prevalent on the edges of the singleleaf pinyon-Utah juniper stands and occurs in large, pure stands in the RNA. Curl-leaf mountain mahogany can range from a shrub when young or in harsh environments, to medium-sized trees when mature. The trees within the RNA are in the latter category, being mostly single stemmed trees 4"-12" dbh and 15'-25' tall. Utah juniper is present throughout the RNA, but is rarely dominant and doesn't achieve the large stature found in other parts of CIRO.

Limber pine (*Pinus flexilis*) and lodgepole pine (*Pinus contorta*) are also present in the RNA, mainly along the upper slopes and ridge. Lodgepole pine never achieved a large stature, but several of the limber pines are large (Table 2). One sub-alpine fir tree (*Abies lasiocarpa*) was found in the western part of the RNA, but is small measuring 3" dbh and approximately 14' tall. Quaking aspen (*Populus tremuloides*) are found mainly along the drainage in the western part of the RNA. Some stands are well developed, with trees 4-10" dbh and 20'-30' tall, but most are in small patches associated with the creek and springs in the area.

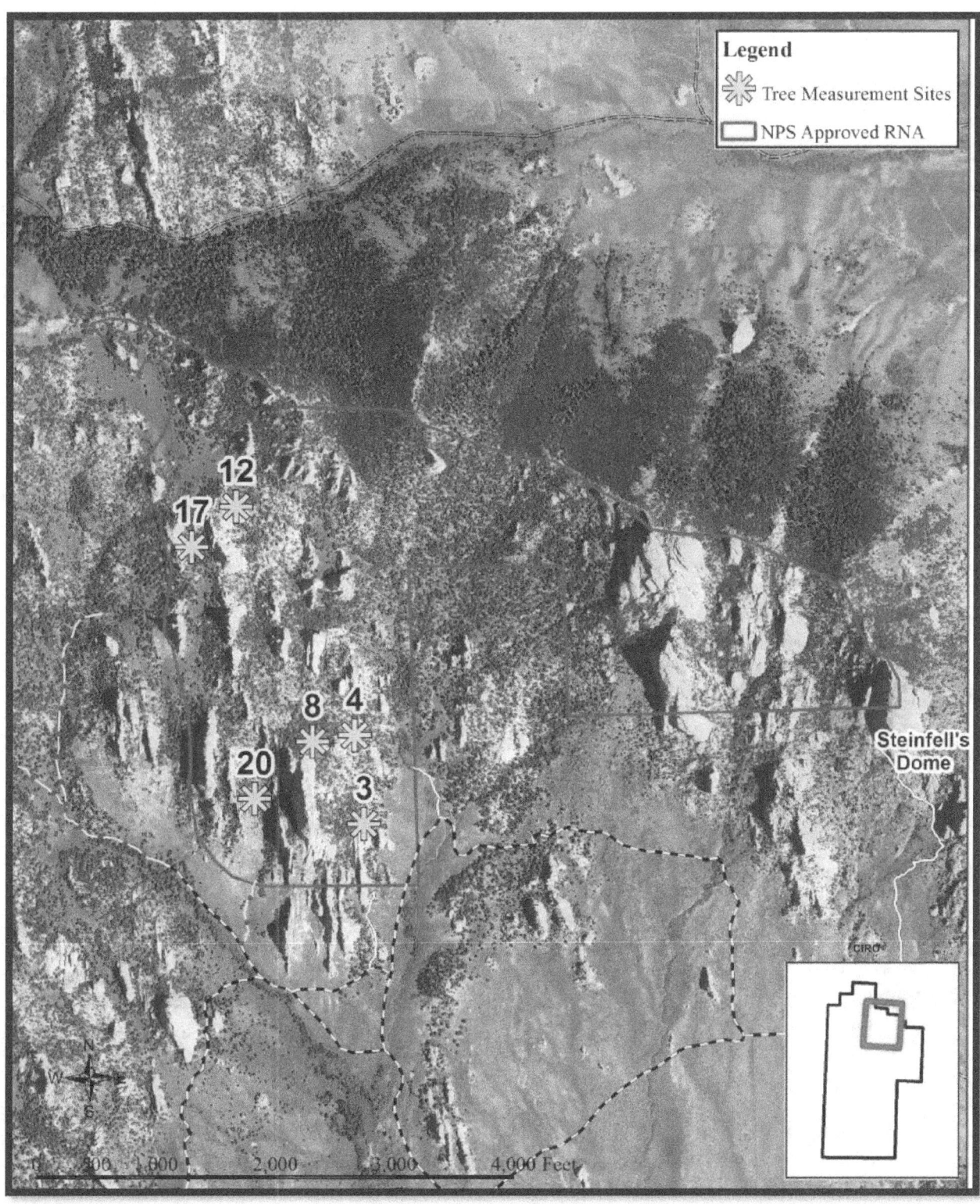

Figure 13. Map of tree measurement locations in the RNA labeled by assessment point number with accompanying photographs on the following page.

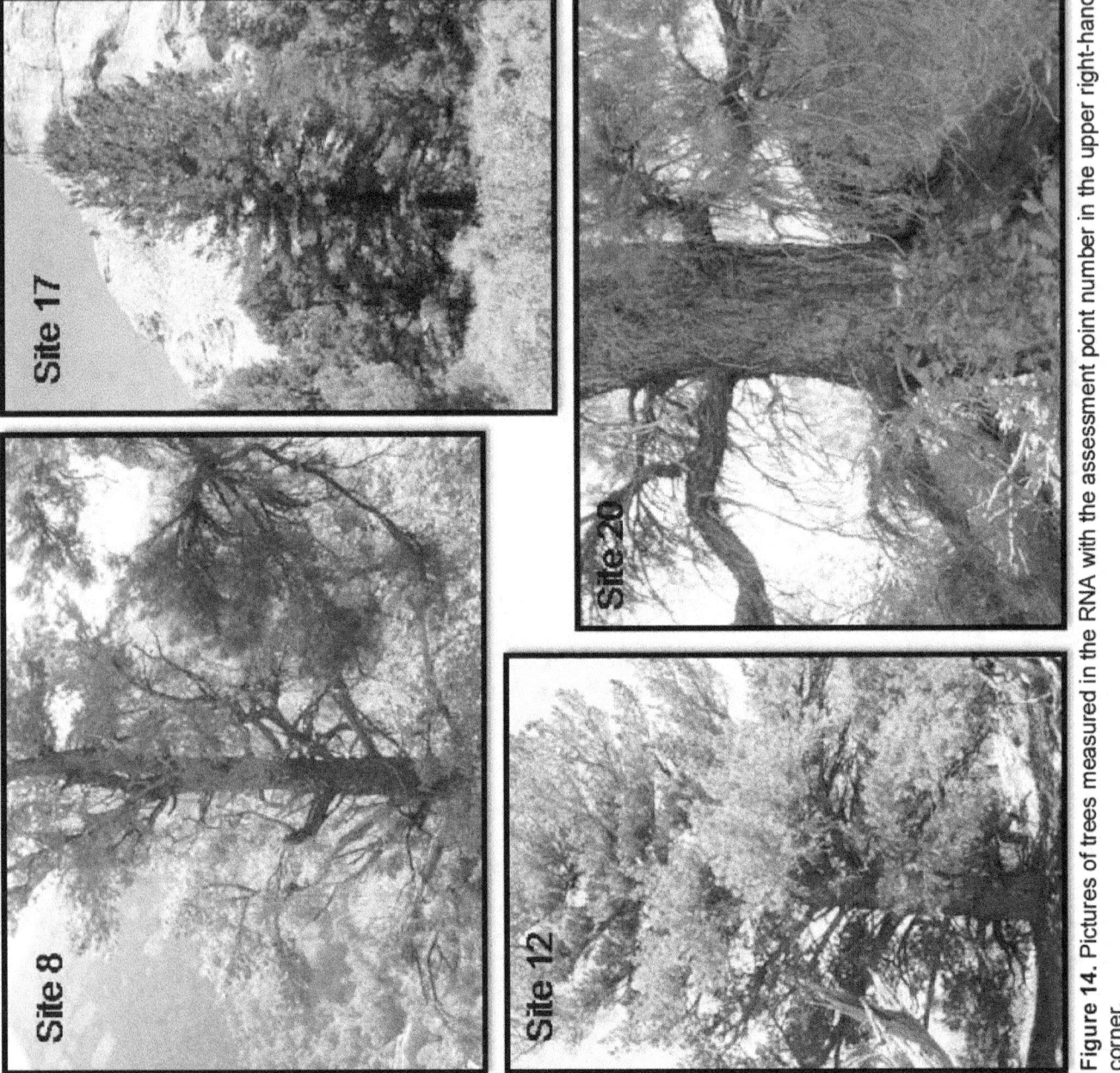

Figure 14. Pictures of trees measured in the RNA with the assessment point number in the upper right-hand corner.

Wildlife

Several mule deer were seen in the RNA during the inventory. Sightings of blacktail jackrabbits (*Lepus californicus*) and mountain cottontail (*Lepus townsendi*) were common. Scat from moose (*Alces alces*), elk, coyote (*Canis latrans*), bushytail woodrat (*Neotoma cinerea*), and various small rodents were observed. Habitat for bats was available in the shelter of the rocks, but no roosting areas were observed. The RNA is very good habitat for mountain lion, but no direct signs were observed. The only reptiles seen during the inventory was the northern sagebrush lizard (*Sceloporus graciosus* spp. *graciosus*).

The warm weather during the inventory was not the best time to observe birds, but a number of common birds were sighted during the surveys. Those recorded included turkey vulture, northern harrier, red-tailed hawk, American kestrel, mourning dove, rock dove, common nighthawk, northern flicker, western kingbird, pinyon jay, black-billed magpie, common raven, violet-green swallow, cliff swallow, mountain chickadee, rock wren, house wren, blue-gray gnatcatcher, American robin, chipping sparrow, brewer's Sparrow, brewer's blackbird, and a possible sighting of a short-eared owl. Several raptors were noted perching on the tall rock outcrops or gliding over the RNA. Turkey vultures were abundant during the survey.

Human Impacts

Very little in the way of human impacts were noted directly within the RNA. Two old fence lines were located in the western part of the RNA (Figure 15). One was approximately at the western boundary of section 19 between the old BLM and US Forest Service jurisdiction (Assessment Point 13) and the other was just to the east. These fences were not maintained and the one on the section line was totally down. No mining or other human activities were observed in the RNA.

Cattle use on the eastern part of the RNA was minimal. Active grazing allotments are adjacent to the RNA with no fence along the boundary. Minimal use was noted in the sagebrush grassland, under the aspen stands, and along the unnamed creek. The greatest impacts were found in the western part of the RNA on the lands previously under USFS management. This area is very well vegetated with a mixed shrub-grass community with well established tree encroachment. A sizable spring-fed wet meadow complex contained willow (*Salix* sp.) and quaking aspen as well as wetland plants such as rushes (*Juncus* spp.) and sedges (*Carex* spp.) were common in the standing water (Figure 16). The area was substantially grazed by cattle that apparently traveled up from the North Fork Circle Creek, where no fenced boundary exists. There was also grazing down the small drainage to the south heading towards the North Fork Circle Creek.

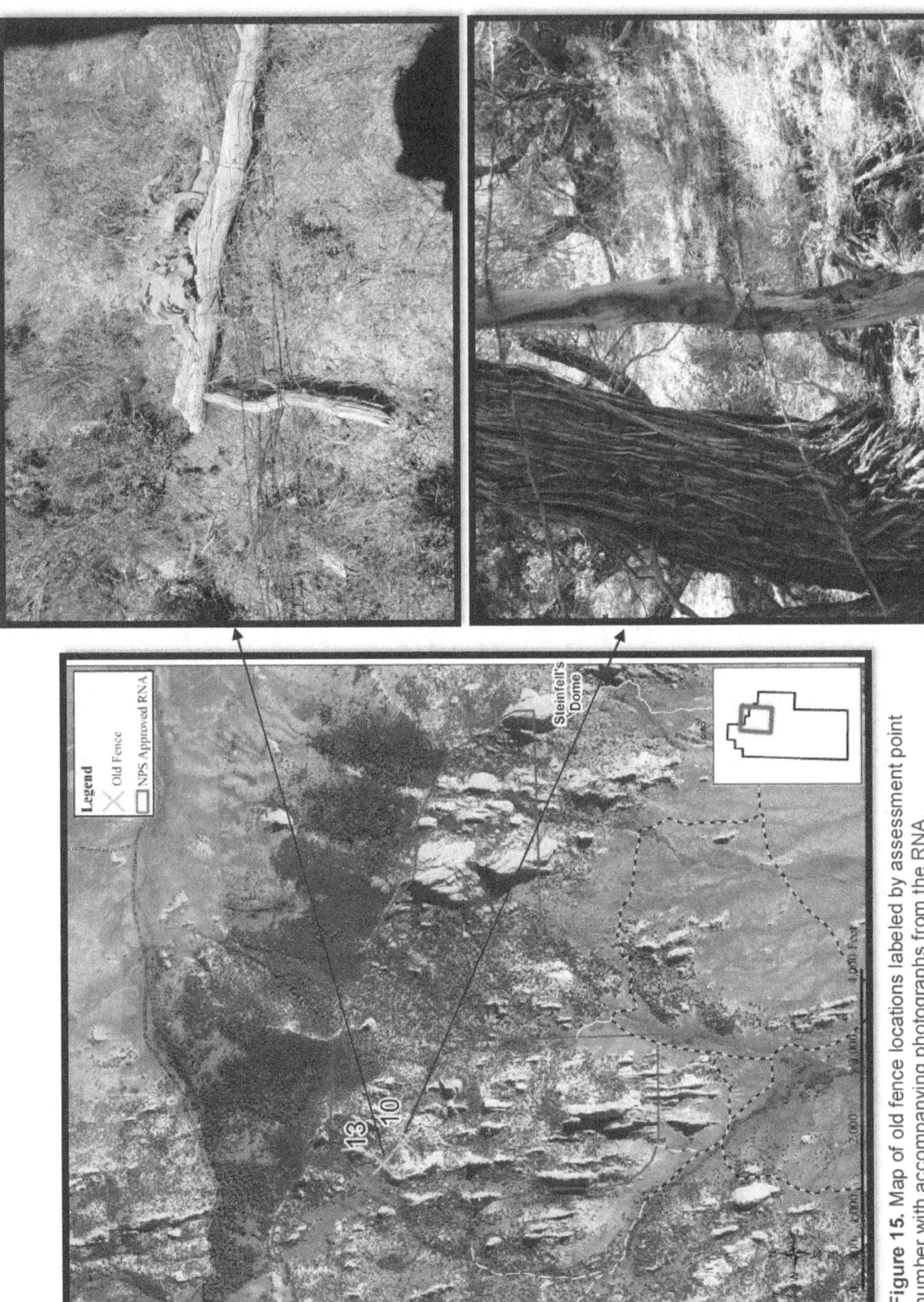

Figure 15. Map of old fence locations labeled by assessment point number with accompanying photographs from the RNA.

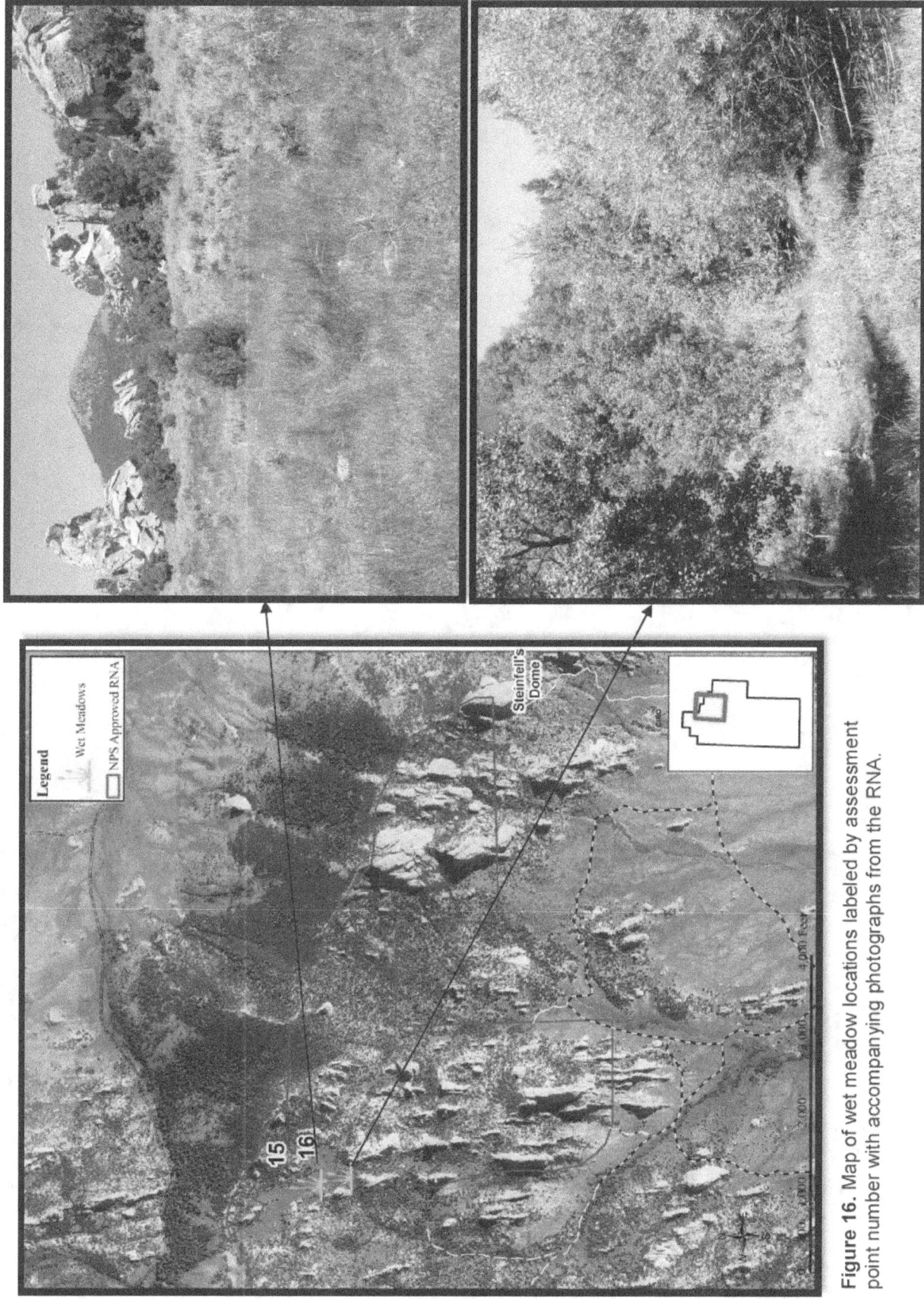

Figure 16. Map of wet meadow locations labeled by assessment point number with accompanying photographs from the RNA.

Recreation uses are very popular for many of the 80,000 visitors to CIRO each year. In a recent study on visitor use, rock climbing (53%) was the main individual reason for visitors using CIRO (Manni et.al. 2009). The next 3 most common recreation uses were general sightseeing (26%), camping (9%), and hiking (5%). The remaining recreation uses each accounted for less than 3% use. To the south and west of the RNA are major trails and rock climbing areas (Figure 16). Hiking, biking, and horseback riding trails lead to the south boundary of the RNA, which is not physically marked on the ground. Steinfell's Dome is a popular climbing rock that lies on the southeast boundary of the RNA. The North Fork Circle Creek Trail is popular with hikers and horseback riders because it leads to the Indian Grove Spring backcountry campground and Graham Peak, the highest point in CIRO.

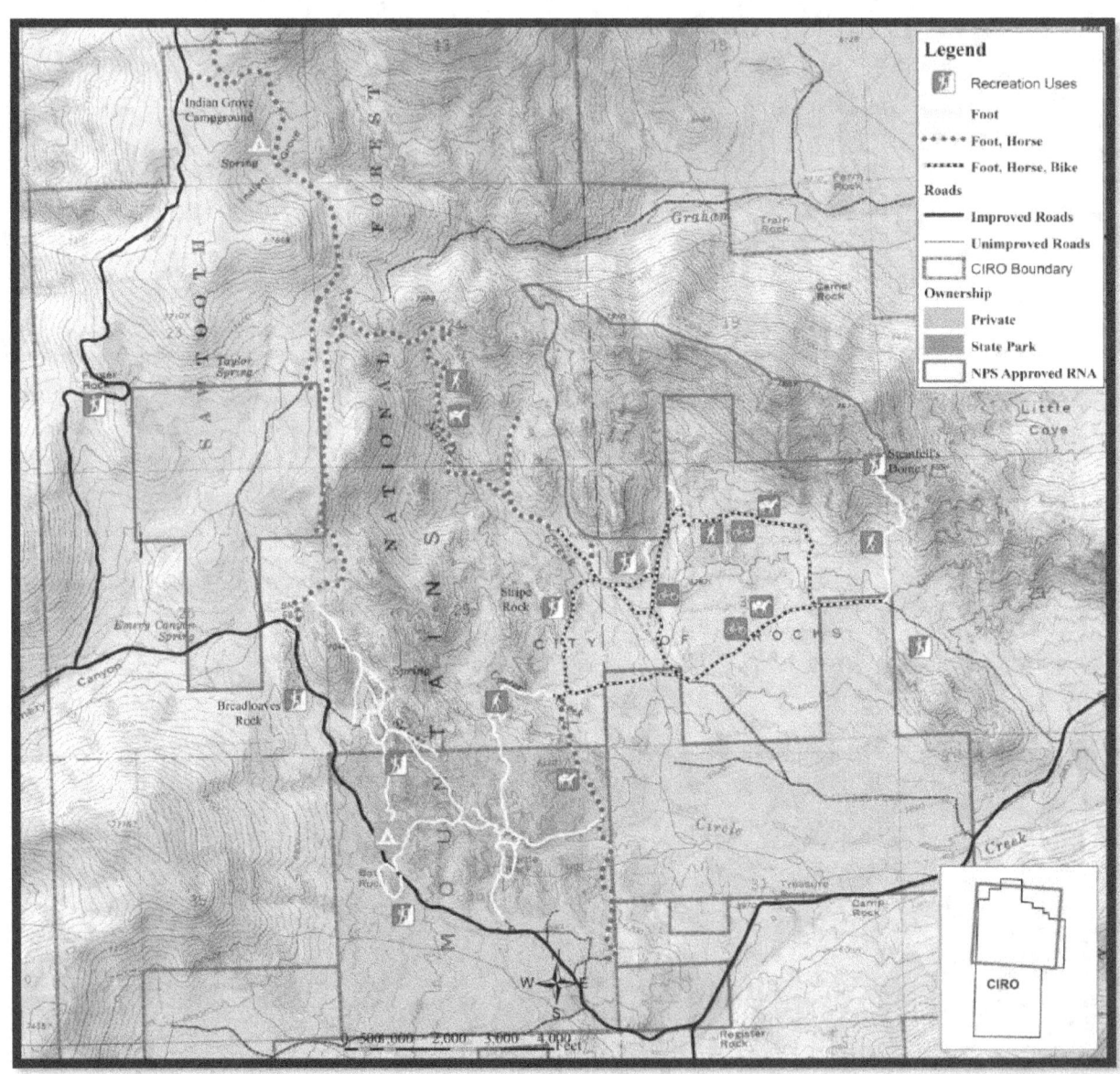

Figure 17. Map of recreation uses around the RNA.

Discussion

The City of Rocks RNA was established in 1985 prior to the City of Rocks inclusion within the National Park System (NPS) as a National Reserve in 1988. A stated goal of the NPS RNA program is to include as many different major habitat types in a relatively un-altered condition, for use as reference sites, as is feasible (NPS 2004). The two stated justifications for the CIRO RNA were the outstanding geologic formations and the undisturbed pinyon-juniper plant community, in particular, the singleleaf pinyon forests that were not represented within Idaho's inventory of RNAs at that time. The CIRO RNA now represents one of four RNA's in Idaho that have a singleleaf pinyon community.

Vegetation
Of these 4, the CIRO RNA is the most developed singleleaf pinyon community (Rust 1996) and may be the best representative of this plant community in Idaho. This study documented 211 plant species in the RNA in a relatively short time period out of the 531 species currently listed for CIRO. The draft vegetation mapping from 2009 shows the RNA to contain 9 plant associations/alliances representing 4 major dominant species; limber pine, singleleaf pinyon, curl-leaf mountain mahogany, and mountain big sagebrush. The proper functioning assessment indicated the biologic integrity landscape attribute is in very good condition along with proper functioning soil and hydrologic landscape processes. Both singleleaf pinyon and limber pine are in mature status (> 200 years old) and show no signs of decadence or disease. The singleleaf pinyon community in the RNA meets the definition for being classified as an old growth stand (Miller et.al. 1999). Old growth stands of pinyon-juniper are rare and structurally complex with higher levels of biological diversity (Miller et.al. 1999).

Wildlife
The wildlife species noted during the field inventory are representative of those found in CIRO. Rodhouse et.al. (2009) documented 35 species of mammals in CIRO, which included 11 species of bats. The rock outcrops and old growth forest of the RNA would be considered good roosting habitat for bats. Sagebrush communities in CIRO are considered possible habitat for pygmy rabbits (*Brachylagus idahoensis*), listed as threatened by the U.S. Fish and Wildlife Service, however to date they have not been documented in the park. The cliff faces and large conifers in the RNA provide nesting and roosting habitat for many species of birds, including raptors and woodpeckers. The old growth singleleaf pinyon/Utah juniper stands provide important habitat for cliff chipmunk and pinyon mouse, both obligate species found on the northern periphery of their range in southern Idaho (Rodhouse et.al. 2010).

Human Impacts
The majority of the CIRO RNA has been undisturbed by human-related impacts. The only man-made structure within the RNA is an old unmaintained fence running north-south along the former boundary between USFS and BLM lands. The RNA is considered separated from the adjacent active grazing allotments by natural barriers. Cattle grazing is occurring in a few areas along the western and southern boundaries, but did not significantly affect the landscape ratings for biotic, soil, or hydrologic processes. Several maintained recreation trails (hiking, biking, and

horseback riding) are also near the western and southern boundaries but there was no evidence of their use extending into the RNA. No obvious signs of rock climbing or other recreation activities were noted during the field inventory.

Recommendations

The CIRO RNA in its current state continues to meet the purpose for which it was originally established. The NPS has 6 major objectives for RNA's (NPS 2004):

1. Preserve a wide range of undisturbed, representative areas that typify important forest, shrubland, grassland, alpine, wetland, and similar natural situations, that have special or unique characteristics, or provide outstanding examples of geological, biological, or ecological processes of scientific interest and importance.

2. Preserve and maintain genetic diversity.

3. Protect against deleterious environmental disturbance.

4. Provide student and professional education.

5. Serve as baseline areas for measuring long-term ecological changes.

6. Serve as control areas for comparing results from manipulative research conducted elsewhere.

The CIRO RNA can meet the objectives stated above with proper management. The RNA is an excellent reference site for monitoring the effects of management actions in similar areas outside the RNA. It also could provide baseline data for long-term monitoring of natural changes, such as wildfire and climate change, in the singleleaf pinyon community. The RNA preserves a healthy old-growth stand of singleleaf pinyon at the northern most distribution of the species and associated community. Species and communities on the northern and southern edge of their distribution provide important areas to monitor for impacts from climate change (Sachiko et.al. 2009). The RNA will also preserve the genetic diversity of the singleleaf pinyon community.

Management of the RNA under the current conditions poses several challenges. RNAs are required to have no activities that "…lessen the site's integrity or permit interference with ongoing research projects" (NPS 2004). Examples of activities that meet this criterion are camping, trail construction, vegetation management, range and pasture use, and mineral entry. Boundaries may be posted or fenced to prevent unauthorized uses. During establishment of RNA, the steep slopes and small amounts of palatable forage over most of the site was considered a deterrent to cattle grazing. Results from this investigation show there are areas in the RNA that will require fencing or other remedies to exclude grazing. The boundaries of the RNA are not posted or fenced on the ground. The only recognizable feature defining the boundary is the ridge between Graham and Circle Creeks forming the north boundary of the RNA.

Cattle grazing in the RNA is the only restricted activity documented by this investigation and actions should be taken to remedy the situation. Any future activities in the RNA should follow RM#77 (NPS 2004), which specifically states "(A)ny potentially disruptive recreational pursuits should not be allowed in these tracts…" Because of the steep nature of the RNA, trails would be required to access any areas in the RNA on a regular basis for activities such as hiking or rock climbing. Construction of trails and staging areas for rock climbing would be in direct conflict with the NPS guidelines for management of RNA's.

A 100 acre expansion to the west of the current RNA was proposed in the CIRO Comprehensive Management Plan (NPS 1995), but it was not delineated on a map. To date, no expansion of the RNA has been approved. An objective of this study was to consider other areas that may qualify for expansion of the RNA. The map in Figure 18 delineates a 170 acre expansion that possibly meets some of the criteria for establishment of a RNA by NPS. The area is located on the west boundary of the RNA and would follow the ridge on the north boundary to the west for approximately 1200' then turn south until the intersection with the North Fork Circle Creek Trail. The boundary would stay east of the trail continuing south until the intersection of an unnamed spur trail near the southern boundary. The boundary would follow the base of rock outcroppings to the east until meeting the southwest boundary of the current RNA. The proposed expansion area has a similar vegetation composition as the current RNA (Table 4).

The implementation of an expanded RNA will require two major changes to the current management plan. First, the Graham Creek grazing allotment would have to be amended for the reduced acreage and a fence would need to be constructed from the ridge to the southwest corner of the current RNA. A similar action may be required for the current RNA due to the overlap of the RNA boundary with the current grazing allotment boundaries. The second major action would be the closure of the unnamed hiking and horseback riding trail. Along with this action, the site would have to be restricted to most recreational activities, such as rock climbing. The expansion area covers a portion of the acreage originally proposed for the RNA by Bal and Wellner (1979) to the USFS. Further research would be required to determine if the expansion area meets all the requirements for a RNA, such as possible changes to plant communities due to cattle grazing. Expansion of the RNA in this area could also conflict with other management goals and objectives for CIRO not considered in this report.

Table 4. Vegetation classes mapped in the proposed expansion for the RNA from data collected in 2009.

Class Description	# Polygons	Acres	% Area
Pinus monophylla - Juniperus spp./ (Purshia tridentata) Artemisia spp. Woodland Complex	3	8.7	5.1%
Pinus monophylla - (Juniperus osteosperma) / Cercocarpus ledifolius Woodland	8	77.9	45.7%
Populus tremuloides Dry Herbaceous Woodland Complex	3	10.6	6.2%
Populus tremuloides - Juniperus scopulorum Woodland	9	27.7	16.3%
Cercocarpus ledifolius / Symphoricarpos oreophilus Woodland	6	19.5	11.5%
Artemisia tridentata ssp. vaseyana - Symphoricarpos oreophilus Shrubland	4	8.3	4.9%
Artemisia tridentata vaseyana / Mixed Herbaceous Shrubland Complex	2	3.6	2.1%
Bare Rock / Sand / Other Bare Ground	20	14.1	8.3%

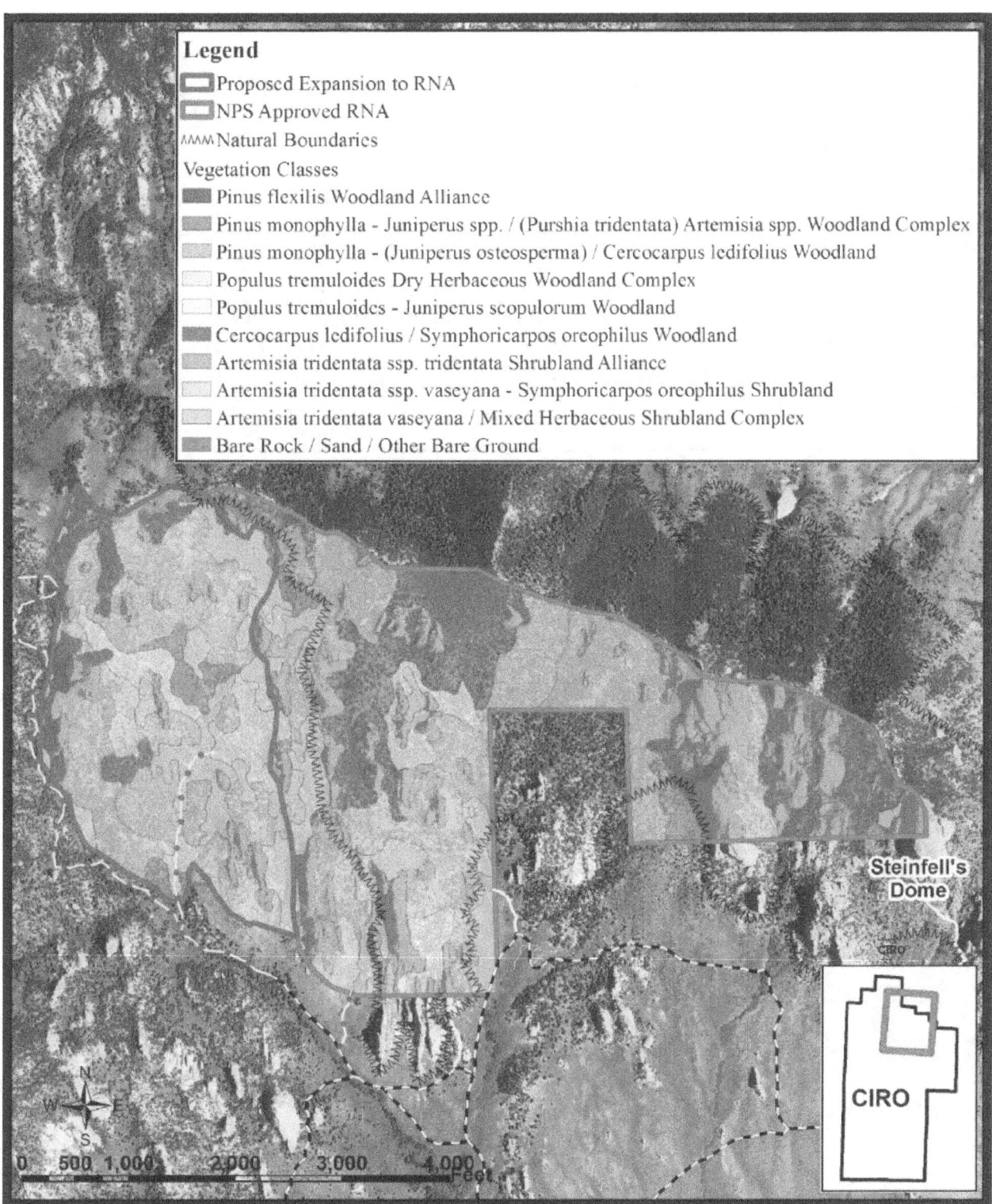

Figure 18. Map of a proposed expansion area to the RNA with vegetation mapping from the vegetation inventory project.

Any areas considered for expansion or adjustment described by section or quarter-section boundaries would require fencing to restrict cattle grazing in the RNA. The natural boundary portions of the Graham Creek and Circle Creek allotments were developed by Upper Columbia Basin Network (UCBN) and CIRO staff based on topographic features visible on a 1:24,000 scale USGS topography maps. The results of our field inventory indicate this boundary does restrict cattle grazing. The current RNA boundary could be adjusted to incorporate the natural boundary of the grazing allotments into the RNA boundary. This would create a 350 acre RNA with a similar vegetation composition (Table 5). Figure 19 is a map showing the current RNA boundary with the proposed adjusted boundary using natural barriers. This adjustment would increase the RNA by 38 acres (12%) and would not require modification to the existing grazing leases. Adjustment of the RNA in this manner could conflict with other management goals and objectives for CIRO not considered in this report.

Table 5. Vegetation classes mapped in the proposed adjusted RNA from data collected in 2009.

Class Description	# Polygons	Acres	% Area
Pinus flexilis Woodland Alliance	3	23.8	6.8%
Pinus monophylla / Juniperus spp. - (Purshia tridentata) Artemisia spp. Woodland Complex	4	12.9	3.7%
Pinus monophylla - (Juniperus osteosperma) / Cercocarpus ledifolius Woodland	9	139.9	40.0%
Populus tremuloides Dry Herbaceous Woodland Complex	1	1.4	0.4%
Populus tremuloides - Juniperus scopulorum Woodland	6	19.4	5.5%
Cercocarpus ledifolius / Symphoricarpos oreophilus Woodland	10	55.9	16.0%
Artemisia tridentata ssp. vaseyana - Symphoricarpos oreophilus Shrubland	3	1.4	0.4%
Artemisia tridentata vaseyana / Mixed Herbaceous Shrubland Complex	2	2.2	0.6%
Bare Rock / Sand / Other Bare Ground	55	92.7	26.5%

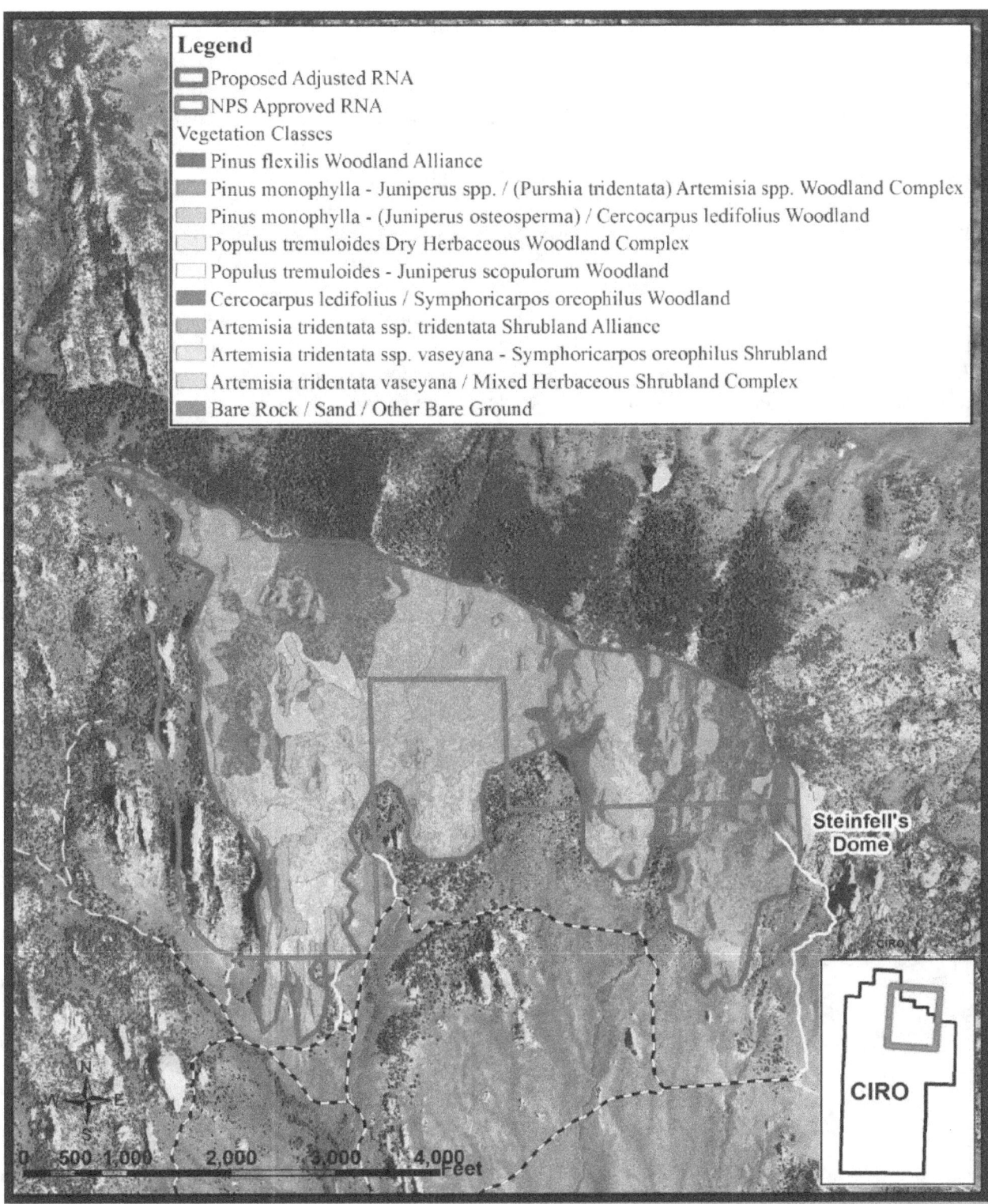

Figure 19. Map of a proposed adjustment to the RNA based on grazing allotment natural boundaries with vegetation mapping from the vegetation inventory project.

Another area considered for expansion is the area north of the RNA. The boundary of the expansion is the ridge line between Graham and Circle Creeks, the north boundary of the RNA, and the natural boundary portion of the Graham Creek allotment in Graham Creek basin. The expansion area occupies approximately 227 acres of steep slopes with an undulating north-facing aspect (Figure 20). The area was not inventoried for this report but the vegetation was mapped and sampled during the 2009 vegetation inventory project. The steep slopes and dense vegetation restricts cattle grazing within the area. The expansion area has a different vegetation composition than the current RNA (Table 6). The majority of the expansion area is equally dominated by Douglas fir (*Pseudotsuga menziesii*)/Rocky Mountain maple (*Acer glabrum*) (48%) and curlleaf mountain mahogany/mountain snowberry (42.8%) with very few exposed rock outcrops (2.0%). The expansion area is undisturbed and could be representative of old growth Douglas fir and curlleaf mountain mahogany associations. This expansion would increase the RNA by 227 acres (72%) and would not require modification to the existing grazing leases. Additional information would be required to complete Form 10-229 to designate the expansion as a RNA (NPS 2004). The expansion could conflict with other management goals and objectives for CIRO not considered in this report.

Table 6. Vegetation classes mapped in the proposed expansion area north of the RNA from data collected in 2009.

Class Description	# Polygons	Acres	% Area
Pinus flexilis Woodland Alliance	2	2.2	1.0%
Pinus monophylla / Juniperus spp. / Mixed Herbaceous Woodland Complex	2	2.4	1.0%
Pinus monophylla - (Juniperus osteosperma) / Cercocarpus ledifolius Woodland	10	10.1	4.4%
Pseudotsuga menziesii / Acer glabrum Forest	8	109.1	48.0%
Cercocarpus ledifolius / Symphoricarpos oreophilus Woodland	14	97.2	42.8%
Artemisia tridentata ssp. vaseyana - Symphoricarpos oreophilus Shrubland	3	1.9	0.8%
Bare Rock / Sand / Other Bare Ground	13	4.5	2.0%

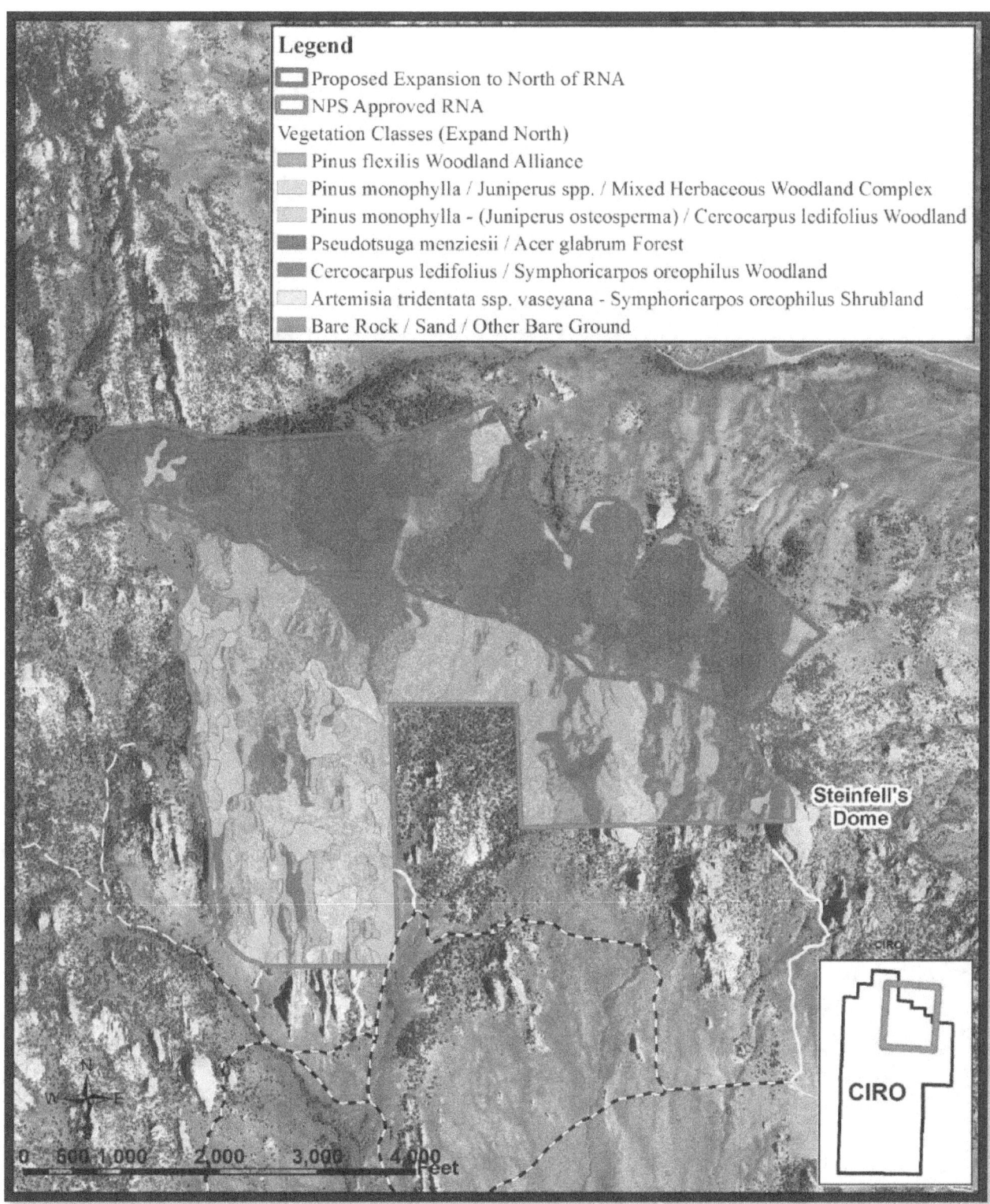

Figure 20. Map of a proposed expansion area north of the RNA with vegetation mapping from the vegetation inventory project.

49

Literature Cited

Anderson, A. L., September 1931, Geology and mineral resources of eastern Cassia County, Idaho, Idaho Bureau of Mines and Geology Bulletin, no. 14.

Bal, J. C. and C. A. Wellner. 1979. Establishment report for City of Rocks Research Natural Area within the Sawtooth National Forest Cassia Count, Idaho. The Nature Conservancy. San Francisco, CA. 25 p.

Bureau of Land Management (BLM). 1987. BLM Amendment to the 1985 Cassia Resource Management Plan. U.S. Department of the Interior, Bureau of Land Management. Burley, ID.

Caicco, S. L. and C. A. Wellner. 1983. Research natural area recommendation for City of Rocks, Bureau of Land Management, Burley District, Idaho. The Nature Conservancy. San Francisco, CA. 15 p.

Christopher, J. E (ed). 2008. The gymnosperm database – *Pinus monophylla*. Online: (http://www.conifers.org/pi/pin/monophylla.htm). Accessed December 2009.

Manni, M. F., N. C. Holmes, E. Papdogiannaki, E. R. Barrie, and S. J. Hollenhorst. 2009. City of Rocks National Reserve visitor study. National Park Studies Unit, Report 208. University of Idaho, Moscow, ID.

Miller, R., R. Tausch, and W. Waichler. 1999. Old-growth juniper and pinyon woodlands. In: Monsen, S. B. and R. Stevens, comps. 1999. Proceedings: ecology andmanagement of pinyon-juniper communities within the Interior West; 1997 September 15-18; Provo, UT. Proceedings RMRS-P-9. USDA Forest Service, Rocky Mountain Research Station,Ogden, UT.

Morris, L. A. 2006. Fire history of the City of Rocks National Reserve from 1926 to 2005. Cooperative Agreement No. H8$07010001. Utah State University, Logan, UT.

National Park Service (NPS). 1995. Comprehensive management plan, development concept plan, environmental impact statement: City of Rocks National Reserve. National Park Service, Pacific Northwest Region, Seattle, WA.

National Park Service (NPS). 1996. Resource management plan for City of Rocks National Reserve. National Park Service, Pacific Northwest Region, Seattle, WA.

National Park Service (NPS). 2005. Vascular plant list: City of Rocks National Reserve. National Park Service, Upper Columbia Basin Network. Online. (http://science.nature.nps.gov/im/units/ucbn/inventory/index.cfm#table). Accessed December 2009.

National Park Service (NPS). 2004. Natural Resource Management Reference Manual #77. U.S. Department of the Interior, National Park Service. Washington, D.C. Online: (http://www.nature.nps.gov/rm77/specialdesignations/RNA.cfm). Accessed December 2009.

National Park Service (NPS). 2010. Bird Checklist: City of Rocks National Reserve and Castle Rocks State Park. National Park Service, Upper Columbia Basin Network. Online. (http://science.nature.nps.gov/im/units/ucbn/docs/Reports/Inventory_Reports/CIRO_Bird Checklist_ParkDoc_200802.pdf). Accessed December 2009.

Pellant, M., P. Shaver, D. A. Pyke, and J. E. Herrick. 2005. Interpreting Indicators of Rangeland Health. Technical Reference 1734-6. U.S. Department of the Interior, Bureau of Land Management, Denver, CO. 122 pp.

Pogue, K. R. 2008. Etched in stone: the geology of City of Rocks National Reserve and Castle Rocks State Park, Idaho. Idaho Geological Survey, Information Circular 63. University of Idaho, Moscow, ID.

Pyke, D. A., J. E. Herrick, P. Shaver, and M. Pellant. 2002. Rangeland health attributes and indicators for qualitative assessment. Journal of Range Management. 55:584-297.

Rodhouse, T. J., E. Madison, K. Oelrich, and L. K. Garrett. 2009. Mammal inventory of City of Rocks National Reserve 2003. Natural Resource Technical Report NPS/UCBN/NRTR— 2009/198. National Park Service, Fort Collins, CO.

Rodhouse, T. J., R. P. Hirnyck, and R. G. Wright. 2010. Habitat selection of rodents along a piñon-juniper woodland-savannah gradient. Journal of Mammalogy, 91(2):000-000.

Rust, S. K. 1996. Classification and inventory for conservation and management of pinyon-juniper ecosystems. Conservation Data Center. Idaho Department of Fish and Game.

Sachiko, Y. G., R. C. Van Der Marel, and B. M. Starzomski. 2009. Climate change and conservation of leading-edge peripheral populations. Conservation Biology, 23(6): 1369-1373.

Sanders, K. D., S. C. Bunting, and R. G. Wright. 1996. Development of a grazing management plan for City of Rocks National Reserve. Subagreement No. 14 to Cooperative Agreement No. CA-9000-8-0005. University of Idaho, Moscow, ID.

Shive, J. P., and C. R. Peterson. 2009. Herpetological inventory of City of Rocks National Reserve 2001. Natural Resource Technical Report NPS/UCBN/NRTR— 2009/200. National Park Service, Fort Collins, CO.

U.S. Forest Service (USFS). 1987 USFS Sawtooth National Forest Land and Resource Management Plan. U.S. Department of Agriculture, Forest Service. Burley, ID.

Wellner, C.A., and F.D. Johnson, compilers. 1974. Research natural area needs in Idaho: A first estimate. Report of the Natural Areas Workshop, April 24-25, 1974, Boise, Idaho. University of Idaho, College of Forestry, Wildlife and Range Sciences, Moscow, ID. 179 p.

Appendix A – List of NRCA Geodatabase Data by Theme

Theme	Layer Name
Air Resources	
Animal	
Geography	
Roads	ciro_roads
Trails	ciro_trails
Historic Trails	historic_trails
CIRO Research Natural Area	ciro_rna_bndy
CIRO Research Natural Area 1K Buffer	ciro_rna_bndy_1kbuffer
CIRO Research Natural Area Adjustment	ciro_rna_bndy_adjusted
CIRO Research Natural Area Expansion	ciro_rna_bndy_expansion
CIRO Research Natural Area Expansion North	ciro_rna_bndy_expansion_north
CIRO Research Natural Area Original	ciro_rna_bndy_original
RNA Assessment Points	joda_rna_sample_points
CIRO Park Boundary	ciro_bndy
Public Land Survey System (PLSS) Sections	Sections
PLSS Townships	Townships
Cities	cities
Land Ownership	ciro_owner
Geogrpahic Features	geographic_feature_names
Geology	
Geology	jgeology_polygon
Soils	ciro_soils
Land Process	
Landuse	
Grazing Allotments	ciro_grazing_allotments
RNA - Southern Idaho	rna_pinyon_juniper_idaho
Plant	
Vegetation in RNA	ciro_rna_veg
Vegetation in RNA Expansion	ciro_rna_expand_veg
Vegetation in RNA Adjustment	ciro_rna_veg_adjusted
Vegetation in RNA Expansion North	ciro_rna_expand_north_veg
Stressors	
Wildfire Boundaries	ciro_all_fires
Water Resources	
Watershed Basin - 6th HUC	ciro_basins
Subwatershed - Circle Creek	ciro_circlecreek_basin
Springs	ciro_springs
Streams	ciro_streams
Raster Data	
Digital Elevation Model	ciro_dem
Hillshade	ciro_hlsd
Digital Raster Graphics (Topographic Map)	ciro_drg.sid
Color Aerial Imagery - 2006	ciro_naip_2006
Color Aerial Imagery - 2009	ciro_naip_2009

Appendix B – Landscape Indicator Scores by Plot for Rapid Condition Assessment

Plot No.	Park Unit	Ecological Reference Code	Soil Name	1. Rills	2. Waterflow	3. Pedestal	4. Bare	5. Gullies	6. Wind	7. Litter	8. Soil Surface	9. Soil Degradation
1	RNA	R025SY018ID	Ola/Earcree	S-M	S-M	S-M	S-M	N-S	N-S	N-S	S-M	S-M
2	RNA	R025SY018ID	Ola/Earcree	S-M	S-M	S-M	S-M	N-S	N-S	N-S	S-M	S-M

Continued

Plot No.	Park Unit	Ecological Reference Code	Soil Name	10. Plant Canopy Cover	11. Compaction	12. Function Structure	13. Plant Mortality	14. Litter Amount	15. Annual Production	16. Invasive Species	17. Reproduction
1	RNA	R025SY018ID	Ola/Earcree	N-S	N-S	N-S	N-S	N-S	S-M	S-M	N-S
2	RNA	R025SY018ID	Ola/Earcree	N-S	N-S	S-M	N-S	N-S	N-S	M	N-S

Appendix C – List of Plant Species at NRCA Upland Assessment Points

Species Name	Growth Form	Non-Native	Aerial Cover by Plot 1	Aerial Cover by Plot 2
Pinus monophylla	tree			3
Cercocarpus ledifolius	tree			1
Artemisia tridentata ssp. vaseyana	shrub		28	18
Chrysothamnus viscidiflorus	shrub		2	2
Purshia tridentata	shrub		5	1
Vulpia octoflora	shrub		T	
Holodiscus dumosa	shrub			1
Pseudoroegeneria spicata	grass			2
Agropyron desertorum	grass		4	
Bromus tectorum	grass	X	2	15
Hesperostipa comata	grass		10	
Leymus cinereus	grass		T	4
Poa pratensis	grass		2	
Poa secunda	grass		2	1
Elymus lanceolatus	grass		2	
Phacelia hastata	forb		2	T
Balsamorhiza sagittata	forb		10	3
Colomia linearis	forb		1	
Chaenactis douglasii	forb			T
Lupinus argenteus	forb		3	2
Alysum desertorum	forb		T	
Chenopodium sp.	forb		T	
Cryptantha ambigua	forb		T	T
Machaexanthera canescens	forb			1
Opuntia polyacantha	forb		T	
Epilobium brachycarpum	forb	X	T	
Descurania richardsonii	forb	X	T	
Sisymbrium altissimum	forb	X	1	

NPS 003/101512, March 2010